Great Settings

Great Settings

PERI WOLFMAN AND CHARLES GOLD

PHOTOGRAPHS BY CHARLES GOLD

CLARKSON POTTER/PUBLISHERS

NEW YORK

To our four sons and our other favorite guests,
for their capacity to enjoy good food and great settings . . .
with the right mix of abandonment and restraint!

PUBLISHED BY CLARKSON N. POTTER/PUBLISHERS, 201 EAST 50TH STREET, NEW YORK,
NEW YORK 10022. MEMBER OF THE CROWN PUBLISHING GROUP.

RANDOM HOUSE, INC. NEW YORK, TORONTO, LONDON, SYDNEY, AUCKLAND

http://www.randomhouse.com/

CLARKSON N. POTTER, POTTER, AND COLOPHON ARE TRADEMARKS OF CLARKSON N. POTTER, INC.
PRINTED IN CHINA

Design by Jennifer Napier

LIBRARY OF CONGRESS CATALOGING-IN-PUBLICATION DATA IS AVAILABLE UPON REQUEST.

ISBN 0-517-70106-5

10 9 8 7 6 5 4 3

contents

acknowledgments

ALTHOUGH THIS BOOK WAS PHOTOGRAPHED BY CHARLEY AND WRITTEN BY PERI, THE RECIPES AND THE SETTINGS ARE THE RESULT OF THE COLLABORATION AND GENEROUS EFFORTS OF OUR MANY TALENTED FRIENDS. THEIR CONTRIBUTIONS BROUGHT A RICH DIMENSION AND VARIETY OF STYLE TO THESE PAGES, FOR WHICH WE ARE VERY GRATEFUL. ❈ A GREAT BIG THANK-YOU TO ALL OF OUR HOSTS: SELMA AND JERRY ABRAMOWITZ, GAIL AND HOWARD ADLER, ROSEANN AND BARRY HIRSH, AUDREY AND DANNY MEYER, JULIET AND TERRY MOORE OF THE WHITE HART INN, CORKY AND STEVE POLLAN, TASHA AND JACK POLLIZZI AND LOIS AND BILL ANDREWS OF T.P. SADDLE BLANKETS, PHYLLIS AND CHARLIE ROSENTHAL, CARLENE AND ED SAFDIE, HARRIET AND BERNIE SHUR, SUZANNE SLESIN AND MICHAEL STEINBERG, AND LISA STAMM AND DALE BOOHER. ❈ *GRAZIE* TO PERI'S SISTER LAURIE WAX AND HER PARTNER, MASSIMO TERESI, WHO INTRODUCED US TO THEIR FRIENDS IN

FLORENCE; SUZANNA PITCHER; AND THE GRACIOUS SIGNORA ROSANNA PIOMBINI OF RISTORANTE CUPOLI. ❧ A TOAST TO THE EXPERTS, FOOD, WINE, AND RESEARCH: PAULA FRAZIER, POLLY TALBOT, MARNIE CARMICHAEL, AND CHARLEY'S BROTHER, LEONARD GOLD OF THE NEW YORK PUBLIC LIBRARY. ❧ WE RAISE OUR GLASSES TO LOURDES SANTIN OF SCHIEFFELIN & SOMERSET CO., WHO GRACIOUSLY PROVIDED US WITH THE SPIRITS, WINES, AND CHAMPAGNES FOR ALL OF THE GREAT SETTINGS. ❧ A MILLION KUDOS TO SHARRON LEWIS, THE HEART OF WOLFMAN·GOLD, AND LILY GENIS, ENERGETICALLY FOLLOWING IN HER FOOTSTEPS, AND MY RESIDENT NIECE, DALIA GOLD. ❧ TO ROY FINAMORE, THANK YOU FOR INVITING US TO SHARE YOUR GREAT SETTING, DELICIOUS COOKING, AND FOR BEING OUR TALENTED EDITOR, TOO. TO PAM BERNSTEIN, WHO INTRODUCED US TO ROY. ❧ THANK YOU TO THE REST OF THE CLARKSON POTTER TEAM: LENNY ALLEN, JANE TREUHAFT, ANDREA C. PEABBLES, JANET MCDONALD, JOAN DENMAN, HOWARD KLEIN, AND THE VERY CREATIVE DESIGNER JENNIFER NAPIER. ❧ TO OUR FRIEND AND MENTOR, LEE BAILEY.

introduction

EVERYTHING SIGNIFICANT IN OUR LIVES HAS ALWAYS BEEN ANNOUNCED, CELEBRATED, DISCUSSED, AND ANALYZED AROUND THE DINNER TABLE. OUR MEALS ARE A CELEBRATION OF A GOOD DAY, OR A CONSOLATION PRIZE FOR THE END OF A BAD DAY. OUR LARGE AND COMFORTABLE PINE DINING TABLE IS AT ITS BEST WHEN SET FOR SIX OR EIGHT OF OUR FAVORITE PEOPLE. IT'S SET SIMPLY, REFLECTING THE SEASON AND THE MEAL ABOUT TO BE SHARED. WE DRINK TOASTS TO EVERYTHING—TO EVERY OCCASION BIG AND SMALL, TO EACH OTHER, TO THE COOK, AND ALWAYS TO THE GOOD FOOD AND GREAT SETTING. ❊ WE REALLY BELIEVE THAT YOU CAN'T SEPARATE THE FOOD BEING SERVED FROM THE TABLE SETTING, SO OUR TABLE ALWAYS REFLECTS THE MEAL, THE SEASON, AND THE OCCASION. WHEN SETTING THE TABLE, WE MOST OFTEN START WITH LARGE CERAMIC BUFFET PLATES AND LAYER THEM WITH A DIFFERENT PLATE FOR EACH COURSE: MAYBE AN ENGLISH CREAMWARE SALAD PLATE AND A

Wedgwood drabware dinner plate. Instead of stiffly folding the napkins, we shake out big cotton squares in subtle colors that complement the setting and look inviting on the table. The silverware is well polished, but purposely unmatched. The glasses are a variety of sizes and styles; we use tumblers with stemmed wineglasses, sturdy pressed glass with crystal flutes. Set on the buffet will be vintage glass cake stands, stacked in graduating sizes and filled with cookies and fruit. Hand-painted Italian pottery dessert plates and American ceramic espresso cups with gold handles await the end of the meal. ❀ Whether we are planning an impromptu family supper or a formal dinner party weeks away, we always start with a list of who's coming. Then we think back. What did we serve the last time they had dinner with us? Isn't one of the guests vegetarian? Doesn't someone in the family hate shrimp? ❀ Next we engage in the game of what we would like to cook or, more important, what we would like to eat. Is it a pasta night, a seafood night, a salad night? Whatever we choose, the food we serve is sure to be homey, easy to prepare, and made from fresh, seasonal ingredients. ❀ The final food decision goes hand in hand with what things are at their best in the market that day. Our heads could be turned and our plans changed by plump, gorgeous tomatoes, tiny new potatoes, a very ripe goat cheese, or fresh scallops in the shell. We are sure to buy extra herbs, fruits, and vegetables just because they are too pretty to pass up and will look great in bowls, baskets, or urns on the table. ❀ Our table is set with whatever strikes our fancy. It could be a collection of ironstone pitchers holding fresh herbs, or a long flat basket overfilled with a variety of crusty braided breads. Or seasonal vegetables and fruits: purple and white baby eggplants, a row of green apples filled with candles, or bunches of asparagus tied with ribbon. Charley often says that in our house "today's centerpiece is tomorrow's dinner!" ❈ There are always candles on our table after dark. Candlelight can turn the simplest meal into an occasion, so in the evening, the center of our table may hold a scattering of simple votives, a grouping of fat pillars in clear glass, or a row of low stocky candles set on a long fish platter. We especially like to put candles in unexpected containers, and we have filled these pages with ideas that display candles in new ways, making the candlelight even more magical." ❈ Every dining table is part of a larger setting, whether it is a formal dining room, a cottage living room, an apartment kitchen, a field of grass, or a perennial garden. The most successful table settings take their surroundings into consideration. Color is one element that effortlessly blends the table into its setting. A garden in full bloom requires only the simplest plates and napkins that pick up the colors of the flowers, or remain as neutral as the grass. ❈ While shopping and collecting for your table, keep your surroundings in mind. Choose your tableware to blend with your dining room as carefully as you choose a slipcover for your living-room sofa. Simply stick to a palette that will seamlessly blend your table setting with your room. Then add the secret ingredient: things you love! ❈ We have learned from our own dinners and those at our friends' homes that everyone is most relaxed and has the best time when the food and setting are creative yet comfortable. There are few rules to this informal style of dining: provide plenty of good food and drink, soft lights, and a pretty, inviting table filled with things that reflect your own style. That is the magic of great settings!

fall LEAVES LOOK AS IF THEY HAVE BEEN PAINTED BY HAND. GREENMARKETS ABOUND WITH EARTHY PRODUCE. WE FIND THAT HEARTY FOODS

LIKE STEWS AND ROASTS ARE APPEALING. AND OUR TABLES AND SETTINGS CELEBRATE THE SEASON. ❧ THE PLATES AND NAPKINS WE CHOOSE ARE WARMER HUED, AND OUR GLASSES HAVE STURDY STEMS. THE GIANT CABBAGES THAT LOOK ALMOST TOO IMPOSING TO EAT BECOME THE CENTERPIECES ON OUR TABLES. ❧ IF YOU KEEP AN EYE ON THE COUNTRY FIELDS IN EARLY OCTOBER, YOU CAN PICK PUMPKINS WHEN THEY ARE STILL GREEN. WITH DARK GREEN LEAVES AND TIGHTLY SPRUNG TENDRILS CURLING FROM THEIR STEMS, THEY ADORN OUR TABLE WITH THE ESSENCE OF AUTUMN. ❧ AUTUMN FOOD IS BEAUTIFUL ON GOLD-BANDED DINNER PLATES. WE LIKE BIG, DARK PLAID COTTON NAPKINS OR TEA-DYED DAMASK THAT WE SLIP THROUGH TWIG OR IVY NAPKIN RINGS. PRESSED-GLASS GOBLETS CONTRAST NICELY WITH MORE PROPER CRYSTAL WINEGLASSES. THEN WE FILL OUR TABLE WITH VINES OF BITTERSWEET AND THE LIGHT AND SCENT OF GOLDEN BEESWAX CANDLES.

PUMPKIN TIME

We announce our setting by lining the driveway with jack-o'-lanterns and hanging the split-rail fence with lights—the glow of the candles in the pumpkins and the twinkle of the electric bulbs welcoming guests.

Pumpkins, picked before they turned orange, sit on the scrubbed pine dining-room table, tendrils of ivy entwined among them. It's a casual setting, designed to match a simple soup supper. Buffet plates serve as place mats, remaining on the table throughout the meal. Individual loaves of bread sit on the edges of the wide-rimmed soup bowls. Lace-edged plaid napkins are more inviting when they are unfolded, shaken out, and set loosely next to the plates.

OPPOSITE. *The scrubbed pine table is flanked by terra-cotta pots filled with Kentia paom. The napkins are big squares of glen plaid, edged with cotton lace.*
ABOVE. *Sturdy hobnail pressed-glass goblets from the late 1800s are used for wine.*

15

Escarole Soup with Chicken Sausage

Served with crusty bread and a chunk of cheese, this makes a quick and hearty main meal. You can prepare dried cannellini beans for this, or just use canned.

2 TABLESPOONS OLIVE OIL

6 LINKS OF CHICKEN SAUSAGE

4 GARLIC CLOVES, COARSELY CHOPPED

1 LARGE SPANISH ONION, SLICED

SALT AND BLACK PEPPER TO TASTE

$1/2$ BOTTLE DRY WHITE WINE

6 CUPS CHICKEN STOCK

2 CUPS WATER

5 CARROTS, PEELED AND SLICED INTO $1/2$-INCH ROUNDS

3 CUPS COOKED CANNELLINI BEANS

2 HEADS ESCAROLE, WELL WASHED, TRIMMED, AND COARSELY CHOPPED

PARMESAN CHEESE FOR GRATING

Heat the olive oil in a large, heavy stockpot over medium-high heat. Add the sausage and cook until browned all over. Remove the sausage, cut it into bite-sized chunks, and set aside.

Reduce the heat to medium, add the garlic, and cook until fragrant. Add the onion, season with salt and pepper, and cook until the onion is translucent, about 4 minutes. Add the wine and stir to dissolve any of the brown bits on the bottom of the pan.

Add the chicken stock, water, and carrots, bring to a simmer, and cook for 10 minutes. Add the sausage and cook for 5 minutes, then add the beans and escarole. Cook for 5 minutes, until the escarole is wilted but not overcooked. Check the seasoning and serve with freshly grated Parmesan cheese.

ABOVE. *The American-made ceramic buffet plates in Queen Anne shape stand in as place mats; they are topped by wide-rim restaurantware soup bowls.* LEFT. *Not-yet-ripe pumpkins and tendrils of ivy are arranged to form the centerpiece.*

ABOVE. *Family and friends, both young and older, gather each October in the New England farmhouse to carve the most extensive and fanciful array of jack-o'-lanterns to welcome guests to a covered-dish supper.* OPPOSITE. *The baked apple, in a restaurantware nappy bowl, is tender enough to eat with a delicate coin-silver spoon.*

Orange-Glazed Baked Apples

4 TABLESPOONS UNSALTED
BUTTER, SOFTENED

$1/3$ CUP DARK BROWN SUGAR

$1/2$ CUP CHOPPED WALNUTS

$1/2$ CUP CURRANTS

$1/2$ TEASPOON GROUND CINNAMON

6 MEDIUM GRANNY SMITH APPLES, CORED

JUICE OF 1 ORANGE

2 WHOLE CINNAMON STICKS

RIBBONS OF ORANGE ZEST

Preheat the oven to 350° F. Butter a round or rectangular ceramic baking dish.

Combine the butter, sugar, nuts, currants, and cinnamon, blending well with your fingers.

Fill the center of the apples with the mixture and place in the dish. Pour orange juice over the apples. Add cinnamon sticks and orange ribbons. Bake for about 30 minutes, until tender.

Serve warm with softly whipped cream.

SERVES 6

CHUCK WAGON BREAKFAST

It's not the open plains but a field in the Berkshires, and it's not a chuck wagon but a vintage truck. No matter. This setting reflects the best of the Old West. The key here is abundance. Wooden buckets are filled to over-flowing with pepperberry branches and local apples. There are bales of hay

and a pile of Native American rugs to serve as seats. The generously sized chambray napkins are ringed in leather and stacked high. And the meal—skillets full of scrambled eggs and sausages, a basket heaped with biscuits, a big bowl of home fries with peppers—is simple but hearty. It makes for good eating in the chilly outdoors.

Even without the truck, all of these elements would make a great back-yard breakfast setting.

ABOVE. *A market basket lined with a dish towel contains the bread basket, a bowl of soft butter, and sturdy green glass tumblers of orange juice.* OPPOSITE. *For this spontaneous outdoor setting, the company truck was piled high with chairs, benches, and all the ingredients for a hearty breakfast, then driven to the edge of a field.*

THE GREAT ALL-AMERICAN THANKSGIVING

There is no setting that idealizes fall more than Tasha and Jack Pollizzi's log house. They manage to blend their Northeastern location with their passion for Western collectibles, and they've created a Thanksgiving setting that's a study in contrasts, seamlessly blended.

Instead of a tablecloth or place mats, flat woven baskets are set at every place. Tasha draws upon her collection of turquoise and silver Indian bracelets to serve as napkin rings for the squares of English chintz. Silver serving platters and antique cutlery are set without compromise on the primitive wood table.

A real mix of Western Americana and British tradition comes with dessert. A footed pressed-glass compote takes up very little table surface, leaving room for a heaping plate of brownies, a footed bowl of out-of-season strawberries, and branches of pepperberry.

OPPOSITE. *The formality of a traditional ironstone tureen, silver cutlery, and stemmed glasses is a pleasing contrast to the primitive plank table and stag-horn chandelier.*

RIGHT. *Layers of pattern are interesting and inviting. For each place, a round, dark-stained willow basket holds a Navajo-patterned buffet plate topped by reproduction red English transfer-ware.* OPPOSITE TOP. *Silver platters with beaded edges are piled high with vegetables, wild rice, and roasted quail. A vine picked from the yard catches the late-afternoon fall light.*

LEFT. *Chintz napkins, with the same coloring as the china, pull the whole look together. Tasha used her collection of silver-and-turquoise bracelets as napkin rings, adding a feather for that extra flourish.* OVERLEAF. *For dessert, the buffet is set with the old family coffee and tea service. The strawberries are piled into a white ceramic bowl, with a silver sugar shaker at the ready, and the footed, pressed-glass compote holds a raspberry-strewn crumb cake.*

BELOW. *The nickel silver gravy boat and English carving set of natural horn with silver cuffs and tips look very much at home in this Western setting.*

RIGHT. *The rich color of the butternut squash and apple soup is striking in the red transferware bowls. Small local apples ring the antique ironstone tureen, adding an extra touch that is so appealing to guests.*

ABOVE. *A Native American tribal
basket holds loaves of pumpkin bread,
baked by the Baker's Wife in Great
Barrington, Massachusetts.* RIGHT. *For
dessert, blue transferware plates are set in
the willow baskets.* BELOW. *A vintage
wooden tool box is a practical and attractive way to store and display cutlery.*

A FIRESIDE DINNER

Dinner in the 18th-century house of innkeepers Juliet and Terry Moore is usually a family affair. The Moore children, Spencer and Jenny, cover the fireside table with branches of the famous New England fall foliage. They help scoop out pumpkinlike gourds to hold hard-ware-store plumbers' candles. To them, simple vintage napkin rings look boring, so they've made their own out of braided bread dough.

Juliet finishes the setting with antique silver cutlery, simple red-wine glasses, and a superb mix of brown English transferware dinner plates. And in a perfect example of food as centerpiece, a large platter of artfully arranged meats and vegetables, topped with sprigs of fresh herbs, completes this classic fall setting.

OPPOSITE. *Brown English transferware plates and old English silver cutlery are laid out on a leaf-covered table.* ABOVE. *Orange gourds have been turned on their sides and carved out to hold plumber's candles.*

White Hart Inn Mixed Grill

You can use any combination of vegetables and meats for this mixed grill.

Marinade

$1/2$ CUP OLIVE OIL

$1/4$ CUP LEMON JUICE

$1/2$ TEASPOON POWDERED GINGER

SALT AND BLACK PEPPER TO TASTE

2 GARLIC CLOVES, COARSELY CHOPPED

6 SAGE LEAVES, FINELY CHOPPED

3 SPRIGS OF THYME, LEAVES REMOVED AND FINELY CHOPPED

4 LEEKS, SPLIT AND WELL WASHED

1 POUND ASPARAGUS, CLEANED

1 EGGPLANT, SLICED IN $1/2$-INCH ROUNDS

3 ZUCCHINI, SLICED IN $1/2$-INCH ROUNDS

2 RED BELL PEPPERS, QUARTERED AND SEEDED

2 YELLOW BELL PEPPERS, QUARTERED AND SEEDED

4 PORTOBELLO MUSHROOMS

2 POUNDS BEEF TENDERLOIN

2 POUNDS BONED LAMB LOIN

Combine the marinade ingredients.

Place the vegetables in a large, flat bowl and brush liberally with the marinade. Cover and set aside for an hour. Coat the meat with the remaining marinade, cover, and refrigerate for an hour.

Prepare a grill.

Cook the meat on the hot grill for 5 minutes. Turn it. Add the vegetables to the grill. Continue turning the meat and vegetables until done to your liking. Set the meat on a platter to rest for about 5 minutes before carving thick slices on the diagonal.

SERVES 6

ABOVE. *The grilled vegetables and meats are artfully arranged in rows on a very large brown transferware platter. For serving, there is a bone spoon and an odd hollow-handled silver and steel fork. Sprigs of fresh chives and tarragon add the finishing touch of color.*
LEFT. *A mixed collection of transferware is far more interesting than a matched set—and it's easier to find.*

FIVE SETTINGS

1. Cotton jacquard napkins ringed with ivory bracelets. American ceramic buffet plate and rimmed soup bowl by Brettt; scalloped dinner plate by Barbara Eigen. Dinner fork and spoon are faux pearl and stainless steel, made in France by Jean Dubost. **2.** Contemporary American stoneware by Lyndt-Stymeist on a cotton print tablecloth with matching napkin. The plastic and stainless cutlery is made in France by Scoff. **3.** Ceramic plates designed and made in England by Myrace Boxer. "Baguette" silverplate cutlery made in Asia for the restaurant trade. The French wineglass is vintage. **4.** Wedgwood creamware, Mottahedeh reproduction scalloped-edge dinner plate, and Apilco buffet plate; antique fish eaters and French bistro silverplate knife. The cloth is a Marseilles spread. **5.** Slate "place mat." Japanese ceramic plates and sandblasted glass sake bottle and cup from the restaurant Katana in New York City. French hand-carved mother-of-pearl fish plate.

winter IS THE SEASON TO PULL OUT ALL THE

STOPS IN DECORATING AND CELEBRATING.

THE COLORS TRADITIONALLY USED DURING WINTER

HOLIDAYS ARE BRIGHT AND CHEERY: THE CLEAR RED OF HOLLY

AND CRANBERRIES FOR CHRISTMAS, THE SPARKLE OF SILVER

FOR HANUKKAH, AND THE WARM GLOW OF GOLD FOR NEW YEAR'S. ❋ WINTER PARTIES

TEND TO BE LARGER, MORE FORMAL CELEBRATIONS, AND OUR SCHEDULES ARE MORE

HECTIC THAN AT ANY OTHER TIME OF THE YEAR. SO ADVANCE PLANNING IS A MUST.

IT'S IMPORTANT TO HAVE DINNERWARE ORGANIZED, THE BEST CHINA COUNTED,

GRANDMA'S DESSERT PLATES AT ARM'S REACH, THE WHITE DAMASK NAPKINS LAUN-

DERED, THE STEMWARE SPARKLING CLEAN, AND THE SILVER POLISHED. THEY'RE ALL

GOING TO GET A CHANCE TO GRACE OUR TABLE THIS SEASON. ❋ FOR CONTRAST, WE

COMBINE OUR BEST TABLEWARE WITH THE ELEMENTS OF WINTER: BARE TWIGS AND

VINES, BASKETS OF RED APPLES, BOWLS OF ORANGES STUCK WITH CLOVES, BUNDLES OF

CINNAMON STICKS TIED WITH RIBBONS, AND THE LIGHT OF LOTS AND LOTS OF CANDLES.

DINING IN THE LIBRARY

Suzanne Slesin usually doesn't like crafts, but she was so taken with the pottery of South African artist Clementian van der Walt that she bought every one of van der Walt's designs. Brightly colored, imaginatively patterned, and quite contemporary, they look remarkably at home in her book-lined dining room. The question of what color napkins to use with pottery this strong was solved when Suzy opened a cupboard and found a stash of paper napkins. A vintage luncheonette napkin holder, an odd contraption when empty, is as terrific looking as it is functional when pressed into use. The antique serving pieces on the dessert

table may seem to be the antithesis of the pottery, yet they look great together. It just proves again that good design mixed with a master hand can blend even the most unlikely of objects.

OPPOSITE. *The chairs are a lively mismatch of old wooden desk and side chairs.*
ABOVE. *The simplicity of the glass and ceramic pitchers and glass jelly jar filled with sugar cubes is a good foil for the pottery.*

LEFT. *A vintage 1920s chrome luncheonette napkin holder stylishly serves up stacks of colorful paper napkins.*

OPPOSITE. *The brightly painted pottery by South African artist Clementian van der Walt is combined with a mix of silver and stainless cutlery.* RIGHT. *Part of Suzy's collection of beaded-glass fruit from the 1940s is piled high in antique turned wood compotes—faux dessert.*

LEFT. *A tall marble compote, a pressed-glass cake stand, and an English ironstone butter tray (commonly used as a sales display in English butcher shops) —all filled with desserts—share a small table in the corner of the library.*

BEYOND COCKTAILS

A cocktail party is a winter mainstay, especially when you want to entertain a large number of guests easily. We used the occasion to stage a tasting of single-malt Scotch. Following the guidelines of *Slainte,* the journal of the classic malts society, we selected six malts, one from each of the main

producing regions. The plan was to start with the lightest single malt and continue to the most robust.

In a classic tasting, small amounts of each malt are served neat, with only water in between. As usual, though, we took creative license in our choice of glasses. Instead of the recommended tulip-shaped glasses, we served the malts in a collection of antique sherry glasses. For water to cleanse the palate, there were stacks of French Piccardi glasses.

ABOVE. *A collection of sherry glasses will be used to serve Scotch.*
OPPOSITE. *The big cream pitcher holding Queen Anne's lace was part of an old*
English wash set.

LEFT. *Bone-handled fish forks and knives with engraved silver blades sit on top of classic Wedgwood creamware plates.* ABOVE. *"Going up the ladder," from the lightest to the heaviest malt.* BELOW. *A silver trophy bowl is filled with lemons, some hollowed out to hold sauces for the salmon served after the Scotch.*

AT HOME FOR THE HOLIDAYS

In our home, the holidays are a celebration of the end of a hectic and busy season, and we go all out with rather extravagant and creative table settings. I look to the abundance of the season for inspiration for new twists on standard themes. This Christmas, old cast-iron garden urns caught my fancy.

Charley put the biggest urn he could lift on one of the three tables and I heaped it high with polished red Delicious apples. Smaller urns for the other tables were filled with wheat grass, which is grown in flats and sold at the farmers' market.

For extra tables, we borrowed two long wooden desks from my office. I covered one with solid green silk organza, the other with gold dotted organza. The middle table, our real dining table, I covered with my favorite cloth, a Marseilles bedspread. And in the spirit of Christmas, the season for giving, we tied each napkin with a favor.

OPPOSITE. *A large garden urn packed with oasis is piled high with apples and galax leaves.* ABOVE. *The napkin is tied with ribbon and an antique glass ornament.*

LEFT. *This urn centerpiece is filled with wheat grass and lady apples that were stuck on wooden skewers.* BELOW. *Napkin favors are ready to be placed on the tables.* RIGHT. *For the middle table, I carved out apples to hold votive candles and marched them down the entire length.*

BELOW AND RIGHT. *Golden moon ornaments were favors for adults; for the children, teddy bears with angel wings.*

OPPOSITE. *Stacked pressed-glass cake stands are laden with sugared fruit.*

RIGHT. *To prevent guests from accidentally pulling the silky tablecloths, I tied them down at each leg with big organza bows.*

A FAMILY'S COUNTRY CHRISTMAS

Jonathan stuck cloves into bright red apples to spell out the initials of each family member. Nicholas stacked the individual braided loaves of bread and

wrapped them with gold cord. Roseann tied dark green satin ribbon around the plaid napkins. And for good measure, Barry caught the new and rambunctious Christmas puppy, Lulu, and gave her a napkin bandanna—a pet to match the setting.

On the center of the table, a still life was assembled by gathering birdhouses from bookshelves; fruits, nuts, and bundles of cinnamon sticks from the kitchen; and votive candles from every drawer.

The preparation for Christmas dinner was in full swing at the Hirshes' house, with each family member playing a role.

ABOVE. *Clove-studded apples are used as place cards, spelling each guest's first initial.* OPPOSITE. *The bare pine table is set with dark green chargers and red transferware dinner plates.*

Pork Tenderloin with Beets and Carrots

4 GARLIC CLOVES, SLICED

1/4 CUP OLIVE OIL

2 PORK TENDERLOINS, TRIMMED OF FAT

SALT AND BLACK PEPPER TO TASTE

4 BEETS, PEELED AND QUARTERED

8 CARROTS, PEELED AND CUT ON THE DIAGONAL INTO 2-INCH SLICES

1/4 CUP DARK BROWN SUGAR

1/3 CUP DARK RUM

1 HEAPING TABLESPOON FRESH DILL, CHOPPED

3 GREEN APPLES, CORED AND QUARTERED

FRESH DILL SPRIGS FOR GARNISH

Preheat the oven to 375° F.

In a large skillet, sauté the garlic in the olive oil for about 2 minutes. Season the pork with salt and pepper, add it to the skillet, and brown on all sides. Transfer the meat to a casserole with a cover.

Add the beets and carrots to the skillet and sauté for 2 to 3 minutes. Add the brown sugar, rum, dill, and salt and pepper. Toss together and add to the pork.

Cover the casserole and bake for about 40 minutes, basting several times.

Add the apples and bake for another 10 minutes, until the apples are tender.

Remove from the oven and let rest for 10 minutes. Slice the pork in 3/4-inch-thick diagonal slices. Arrange on a platter surrounded by the vegetables, and garnish with sprigs of fresh dill.

SERVES 4

OPPOSITE TOP. *Beets and carrots stain the tenderloin and blend with the red of the transferware platter. Roseann serves this with garlic mashed potatoes.* OPPOSITE BOTTOM. *Glazed and braided breads look very festive when tied together with gold cord.*

BELOW. *Wired-edge satin ribbon makes beautiful bows for napkin ties.* OVERLEAF. *On the sideboard, an unusual cake stand of clear and frosted glass elevates the pear and ginger upside-down cake, leaving room for silver forks and a goblet of whipped cream. Gold-rimmed glasses with cinnamon sticks await coffee.*

Pear and Ginger Upside-Down Cake

Pears

4 TABLESPOONS BUTTER

$\frac{1}{2}$ CUP FIRMLY PACKED DARK BROWN SUGAR

3 PEARS, PEELED, HALVED LENGTHWISE, AND CORED

Cake

1 CUP ALL-PURPOSE FLOUR

$\frac{1}{2}$ TEASPOON BAKING SODA

PINCH OF SALT

1 TEASPOON GROUND GINGER

$\frac{1}{4}$ TEASPOON FRESHLY GRATED NUTMEG

PINCH OF GROUND CLOVES

1 EGG, BEATEN

$\frac{1}{2}$ CUP FIRMLY PACKED DARK BROWN SUGAR

$\frac{1}{2}$ CUP MILK

$\frac{1}{4}$ CUP MILD MOLASSES

4 TABLESPOONS BUTTER, MELTED AND COOLED

CONFECTIONERS' SUGAR FOR GARNISH

SOFTLY WHIPPED CREAM FOR SERVING

Preheat the oven to 350° F.

To prepare the pears, melt the butter in a small saucepan over medium heat. Add the sugar and stir until it is dissolved. Pour into an ungreased 9-inch round cake pan.

Arrange the pears, cut-side down, in the sugar with the tops meeting in the center.

To prepare the cake, sift the flour, baking soda, salt, and spices into a large bowl.

In a small bowl, combine the egg, brown sugar, milk, molasses, and butter. Stir into the flour mixture, beating just until smooth. Pour the batter evenly over the pears.

Bake 40 to 45 minutes, until a cake tester comes out clean.

Cool in the pan for 20 minutes. Loosen the edges and turn onto a cake plate.

Sift confectioners' sugar over the top. Serve with a dollop of whipped cream.

SERVES 6

WINTER IN FLORENCE

We spent a winter week in Italy, chilled to the bone but sustained by the simple foods, the local wines, and the Florentine way of life. In spite of the cold snap, geraniums were in bloom and rosemary was abundant on my sister Laurie's terrace. In the open markets, stalls were filled with a mix of winter greens and the first crop of basil and fava beans.

The artichokes were like flowers, with long stems and abundant leaves. I couldn't get enough of them, not just to eat, but to use on the table in their untrimmed, uncooked, natural state. Laurie and I encircled pillar candles with the small artichokes, tied them with taffeta bows, and lit the wick. They helped create the perfect natural setting for a typical Northern Italian antipasto of white beans, chopped spinach, and Pecorino.

OPPOSITE. *A sprig of rosemary tucked between napkin and ring is a fragrant reminder that we're in Florence. The blue English Spode dinner plates are a mixed collection.*
ABOVE. *The artichoke centerpieces burn warmly and brightly.*

A LEISURELY LITTLE LUNCH

The winter sun streaming through the window warmed the inviting table, ready and set for *pronzo di mezzogiorno*.

One plaid tablecloth was thrown over another, with the soft green rolled napkins falling over the table's edge. Pottery plates in the same dusty colors are layered one on the other. A big basket of focaccia and rosemary, bowls of olives with sprigs of sage, and a chunk of *parmigiano* are all the basics of any good Italian meal.

ABOVE. *Olives are placed in ceramic and silver bowls. A wedge-shaped cheese chisel is used to break off chunks of* parmigiano. OPPOSITE. *The focaccia is garnished with sprays of flowering rosemary. Richard Ginori ceramic plates are a favorite on the Italian table.*

ABBONDANZA

It was snowing when we went up the hill to Ristorante Cupoli, in a small town just south of Florence. When we stepped inside, it was warm and cozy, with a huge roaring fire. There were carts groaning with the most perfect cheeses and breads, baskets of truffles, bowls of custards, and platters of tarts and biscotti—and a display of grappas the likes of which we had never before seen.

There were only a few other diners on the cold afternoon, and we were treated like family. Our friend Massimo Teresi, who had brought us to this fabulous place, consulted with Signora Piombini on the menu for only a minute.

For starters, a salad of arugula. Ravioli with butter and sage came next, then linguine with thin slices of *tartufi nero*. We couldn't still have looked hungry, but out came a giant roasted chicken.

We drank Spumanti, then red wine. We ate crème caramel and biscotti. We drank grappa and coffee with anisette. The sky had cleared, the sun was going down, and we were happy to be in this great setting.

PRECEDING PAGES. *A clamp-like contraption holds a wedge of* parmigiano *ready for the silver-handled grater* (LEFT). *Ceramic goblets filled with sugar are hand-painted with the crest and name of the restaurant.* BELOW. *Delicate glass bottles of grappa sit on a silver tray.* RIGHT. *The arugula salad, topped with grated* parmigiano, *hides soft, runny* stracchino. *It is circled with bruschetta and polenta.*

Crostini

A platter of crostini and bruschetta is often served as the start to a Florentine dinner.

2 TABLESPOONS OLIVE OIL

1 ONION, FINELY CHOPPED

6 CHICKEN LIVERS

$1/2$ CUP WHITE WINE

1 TABLESPOON CRUSHED CAPERS

1 TEASPOON TOMATO PUREE

CHICKEN STOCK

1 LOAF OF ITALIAN BREAD, SLICED
IN 1-INCH ROUNDS AND TOASTED

Heat the olive oil in a skillet over medium heat. Add the onion and cook until limp. Add the livers and cook them for 4 or 5 minutes, until no longer pink, breaking them up as they cook and soften. Add the wine and cook for 2 or 3 minutes.

Add the capers, tomato puree, and a little chicken stock. Cook for about 15 minutes, adding more stock as necessary to make a thick but spreadable mixture.

Spread on the toast and serve while still hot.

SERVES 6

1

2

3

4

CANDLES

Nothing is more magical on an evening table than candlelight. For special times, it's fun to add fruits, flowers, and vegetables.

1. Wire a bunch of grapes to a silver candlestick, then tie with a gold ribbon or raffia. **2.** Scoop out lemons or limes for votive candles and set them on unusual plates, en masse. Here they are placed on vintage glass plates in the shape of hands. **3.** Fill a basket with small flats of salad greens, then stick slim tapers into the soil. **4.** Encircle a fat pillar candle with pencil asparagus, hold them in place with a heavy rubber band, then tie with a ribbon. **5.** So simple: just find the right size and shape candle to fit into a small cast-iron garden urn. **6.** Place rolled beeswax pillar candles inside glass cylinders half filled with water. Strip the foliage from roses and surround the candles.

5

6

spring

TABLES REQUIRE ONLY THE MOST SUBTLE DECORATION. WITH THE SCENT OF LILACS AND HERBS IN THE AIR, WE ARE INSPIRED TO SET A LIGHTER TABLE USING FRESH YOUNG PRODUCE AND TABLEWARE THAT COMPLEMENTS IT. ❧ YOUNG ASPARAGUS, WITH THEIR PURPLE-TINTED SPEARS, NOT ONLY TASTE LIKE SPRING BUT THEY LOOK LIKE EARLY BLOSSOMS. IT'S OFTEN HARD TO DECIDE WHETHER TO TIE THEM WITH RIBBON AS A CENTERPIECE OR TO EAT THEM ON TOAST WITH MELTED BUTTER. WE DO BOTH! ❧ ARTICHOKES HAVE BEEN COPIED BY ARTISTS THROUGHOUT HISTORY IN PAINTINGS AND CERAMICS. IN THE SPRING, WHEN THEY ARE AT THEIR BEST AND MOST ABUNDANT, WE FILL BASKETS AND BOWLS WITH SMALL ONES. WE HOLLOW OUT GIANT ARTICHOKES TO USE AS CANDLEHOLDERS OR SAUCE BOWLS. ❧ THEN ALONG COME CHIVES. THEIR TUFTS OF PURPLE FLOWERS BLOOM FOR ONLY A WEEK OR TWO—JUST LONG ENOUGH TO BRIGHTEN OUR TABLE ❧ CREAMY CHINA, VINTAGE GREEN-AND-WHITE TRANSFERWARE, OR HANDMADE POTTERY WITH A FAINT COLOR WASH TAKE THE PLACE OF FORMAL DINNERWARE. WE USE FLOWERING HERBS AROUND LARGE PALE COTTON NAPKINS TO MARK THE CHANGE OF SEASON.

AN ARTIST'S PASSOVER

The Passover table, which is full of ceremony and ritual, is never boring at the home of New York artists Selma and Jerry Abramowitz. Selma's style of quirky humor informs both the setting and the meal, without sacrificing any of its traditional elements.

Decorated eggs, which are usually associated with Easter, have artfully become a part of the Abramowitzes' Passover table. Painted to symbolize Jewish biblical characters, they bring charm and wit to the table.

A white damask banquet cloth unifies the three unmatched tables needed for the big holiday gathering. Over the years the Abramowitzes have collected enough Wedgwood drabware for every place setting, but the James Robinson sterling has to be supplemented with kitchen stainless. To make guests feel extra special, Selma personalizes the paper ribbons tied around the napkins.

OPPOSITE. *Double old-fashioned glasses and Wedgwood drabware plates create a modern rather than a traditional setting.* ABOVE. *The name of each guest, in both English and Hebrew, is printed on the paper ribbon napkin ties.*

Selma's Haroset

This is a Moroccan recipe.
Shaping the haroset like pyramids is
a Persian tradition.

2 CUPS WALNUT MEATS

1 CUP BLANCHED SLIVERED ALMONDS

25 PITTED DATES

10 LARGE DRIED FIGS

20 DRIED APRICOTS

$1/2$ CUP SWEET PASSOVER WINE

GROUND WALNUTS,
TO COVER THE PLATTER

GROUND CINNAMON,
TO COAT PYRAMIDS

In a food processor fitted with the steel blade, chop the walnuts and almonds into coarse pieces.

Add the dried fruit, and blend until combined into a rough paste. Mix in just enough wine to make a malleable paste.

Cover the bottom of a platter with ground walnuts, to represent sand. Shape the haroset into pyramids of different sizes.

Sprinkle ground cinnamon on wax paper, and press the flat sides of the pyramids into the cinnamon to completely coat. Place the pyramids on the nut-covered platter. Cover lightly with plastic wrap and refrigerate until an hour before serving.

SERVES 12

OPPOSITE TOP. *The haroset in the shape of pyramids is on a bed of chopped nut "sand."* OPPOSITE BOTTOM. *For the center of the table, eggs painted by Selma to represent Biblical characters rest in cut-out wooden blocks.* LEFT. *The traditional Passover Seder plate holds a roasted lamb shank, roasted egg, haroset, and both sweet and bitter herbs.*

ABOVE. *The torte awaits the end of dinner on a deep, dark cake plate.* RIGHT. *Elijah's hand-painted glass has a place of honor next to the menu, which is in both English and Hebrew.*

Sephardic Orange, Nut, and Date Torte

Selma always serves this recipe from Gloria Greene's Jewish Holiday
Cookbook.

2 LARGE NAVEL ORANGES

1 ½ CUPS BLANCHED ALMONDS, COARSELY CHOPPED

1 CUP SUGAR

¼ TEASPOON GROUND CINNAMON

½ CUP PITTED DATES, FINELY CHOPPED

6 LARGE EGGS

Garnish

1 ORANGE, PEELED AND THINLY SLICED

SUGAR

Place the whole oranges into a medium saucepan and cover with cold water. Bring to a boil, cover the pan, and lower the heat. Simmer for about 40 minutes, or until very soft. Drain the oranges, return them to the pan, and cover them with cold water. Allow them to soak for 5 minutes. Drain well and dry. Cut each orange into 8 wedges and remove any seeds.

Preheat the oven to 375° F. Grease and sugar a 10-inch springform pan.

Place the almonds and ¼ cup of the sugar in a food processor and process until finely ground. Add the cinnamon and set aside. Put the orange pieces into the processor and pulse until coarsely chop-ped. Add the dates and pulse until just blended.

Separate 2 of the eggs. Beat the whites until they form soft peaks. Gradually beat in ¼ cup of the sugar and beat until glossy and stiff. Set aside.

In a large bowl, beat the 4 whole eggs plus 2 egg yolks with the remaining ½ cup sugar until light and fluffy. Stir in the orange-date mixture and the ground nut mixture. Gently fold in the beaten egg whites until blended; do not overmix. Pour the batter into the pan.

Bake for 50 to 60 minutes, or until the torte is browned. Run a knife around the edges to separate the torte from the pan, and cool completely on a rack.

Garnish with thin slices of orange and a sprinkling of sugar.

SERVES 12

A SPRING DINNER IN THE KITCHEN

In this small butter-colored room, a converted butler's pantry off the kitchen, very little is needed on the table to please the eye.

The built-in, old-fashioned breakfront shows off a collection of antique ironstone and creamware. An antique majolica asparagus platter and an ironstone tureen heaped with lemons, both decorative and functional, fill the center of the narrow marble-topped table.

Soup plates filled with a sauce of bright red plum tomatoes and sweet basil over pasta add a splash of color to the setting. Cotton dishtowels, all of the same colors but in a variety of patterns, make practical and generous napkins.

ABOVE. *Hillary peeks out from behind a painted wood ladder-back chair.*
OPPOSITE. *The table is nestled in the converted butler's pantry.*

Tomato Salad Pasta

*A quick and easy cold tomato topping
for hot pasta, this is a delicious way to savor
the first tomatoes of spring.*

24 RIPE PLUM TOMATOES,
PEELED AND CHOPPED

6 GARLIC CLOVES,
FINELY MINCED

SALT AND BLACK PEPPER TO TASTE

$1/3$ CUP OLIVE OIL

3 TABLESPOONS BALSAMIC VINEGAR

1 BUNCH FRESH BASIL LEAVES,
CHOPPED

1 TO $1^1/_2$ POUNDS
OF THIN LINGUINE

In a large porcelain bowl, combine the tomatoes,
garlic, salt, and pepper. Add the olive oil, balsamic
vinegar, and basil. Toss just enough to combine.
Set aside while you prepare the pasta.

Bring a large pot of water to a boil. Salt it well,
add the linguine, and cook until al dente. Drain
the pasta, divide it among serving plates, and top
with the sauce.

SERVES 6

LEFT. *An English fork and spoon rest on a wheat-
pattern ironstone soup bowl. The unmatched goblets
are early 1900s pressed glass.* RIGHT. *The glass
Scottie was made to hold penny candy in the early
part of the 20th century; here it serves butter.*

DINNER FROM THE GREENMARKET

Whatever is seasonal at the Union Square Greenmarket finds its way in one form or another to the dining table of New York restaurateur Danny Meyer and his wife, Audrey.

One early spring morning, the Meyers found a farmer selling speckled eggs with spring-pale tints. They brought back a flat of wheat grass and filled it with candles and pots of baby herbs to place in one of Audrey's many Italian ceramic bowls. And that was just to decorate the table! Fava beans, pale green frisée, and bright yellow peppers made up the crunchy salad. The first rhubarb of the season became a dessert crisp.

When Audrey and Danny travel, they collect not only recipes but all sorts of things for the table. The dinner plates are from many of their favorite Italian country restaurants, each hand-painted with the specialty of the house.

OPPOSITE. *The spring table is a feast of blue and green.* ABOVE. *A flat of wheat grass, with the light of votive candles shining out between the blades, takes center stage.*

ABOVE. *A hand-painted Italian pottery bowl is temporarily planted with potted herbs for one end of the table.* LEFT. *Georg Jensen acorn sterling was passed down from Danny's family, and it's now Audrey's pattern of choice, too.*

Rhubarb Crisp

Using the best fruits of the season, crisps always make a tasty, friendly dessert. In this one, rhubarb says spring. This fine recipe is from The Union Square Cafe Cookbook *by Danny Meyer and Michael Romano.*

$^3/_4$ CUP PLUS 3 TABLESPOONS
ALL-PURPOSE FLOUR

$^1/_3$ CUP BROWN SUGAR

1 $^1/_4$ TABLESPOONS GRANULATED SUGAR

$^1/_8$ TEASPOON GROUND CINNAMON

5 $^1/_3$ TABLESPOONS UNSALTED BUTTER,
SOFTENED

$^1/_2$ CUP COARSELY CHOPPED TOASTED WALNUTS

2 POUNDS RHUBARB,
CUT INTO $^1/_2$-INCH PIECES

$^3/_4$ CUP SUGAR

1 PINT STRAWBERRY OR VANILLA ICE CREAM

Preheat the oven to 400° F.

In a bowl, combine the ¾ cup flour, brown and granulated sugars, and the cinnamon. Work in the butter with your fingers until the mixture is crumbly. Add the walnut pieces.

In a 10-inch pie plate or ovenproof serving dish, toss the rhubarb with the ¾ cup sugar and 3 tablespoons flour to coat evenly. Scatter the crisp topping evenly over the rhubarb. Bake for 35 minutes, until the rhubarb bubbles at the sides and the topping is crisp and brown. Serve warm topped with ice cream.

SERVES 6

THE WELL-EDITED DINNER

Roy Finamore is not only the editor of beautiful and original cookbooks, he is also a superb editor of his own flea-market treasures. Most of Roy's collec-

tions belong on the dining table and go hand in hand with the good, unfussy food he prepares.

Although his dining table is of well-worn country pine, Roy sets it with a sophisticated mix. Mid-20th-century classics are the stars: Russel Wright dinner plates and silver-plate flat-ware, Georg Jensen serving spoons, and Bakelite kitchen cutlery look as if they were meant to be together. Mid-19th-century basics—steel and wood cutlery, ironstone platters, and yellowware crocks—add a more homey touch, creating an inviting and friendly setting.

ABOVE. *Blueberry branches and peach-colored roses are combined in a large glass jug.*
OPPOSITE. *The wineglasses are a mix of old and new pressed-glass goblets.*

Pork Tenderloin in a Fennel Crust

$^1/_4$ CUP FENNEL SEEDS

2 GARLIC CLOVES, MINCED

1 TABLESPOON ORANGE ZEST

SALT AND COARSELY GROUND
BLACK PEPPER

1 TABLESPOON OLIVE OIL

2 PORK TENDERLOINS, TRIMMED

Place the fennel seeds on a cutting board and dampen them with water (this helps keep them on the board); chop coarsely. Combine with the garlic, orange zest, salt, pepper, and olive oil. Rub the mixture over the pork, place in a sealable plastic bag, and refrigerate for 2 to 3 hours.

Preheat the oven to 450° F. Place a baking sheet or low-sided metal roasting pan in the oven while it preheats.

Place the pork on the baking sheet and roast for 18 to 20 minutes, turning it after 10 minutes so it browns evenly. Let rest for 10 minutes before carving into thick slices, or serve at room temperature, carved into thin slices.

SERVES 4

OPPOSITE TOP. *Sour cherry and rosemary focaccia is served on a vintage Palmer Smith hammered-aluminum platter.* OPPOSITE BOTTOM. *Cutlery of many disciplines shares the table: late 19th-century steel and coca wood knives and forks, 1920s Bakelite cutlery in a yellowware crock, and totally modern Russel Wright silver-plate butter knives.* LEFT. *Dinner is set out on old ironstone platters on a side table. Natural beeswax candles and single peonies are from the farmer's market.*

White Bean Puree

2 TABLESPOONS OLIVE OIL

1 GARLIC CLOVE, MINCED

3 SAGE LEAVES, CHOPPED

1 CAN CANNELLINI BEANS,
DRAINED

CHICKEN STOCK

SALT AND PEPPER TO TASTE

EXTRA-VIRGIN OLIVE OIL
FOR GARNISH

SAGE LEAVES FOR GARNISH

Place the oil and garlic in a skillet and cook over medium heat until the garlic is fragrant. Add the chopped sage and cook for a minute. Add the beans and enough stock to barely cover, season to taste with salt and pepper, and bring to a simmer. Cook for about 10 minutes.

Place in the bowl of a food processor and blend until smooth. Spoon the puree out onto a platter, drizzle with olive oil, and garnish with sage leaves.

SERVES 4

LEFT. *Russel Wright "Highlight" dinner plates, milk glass goblets, mixed vintage cutlery, and cotton-dishtowel napkins look comfortable together on the bare wood country table.*

89

Grandma Gorman's Chocolate Cake

*This is a no-nonsense, old-fashioned chocolate cake—the kind
you just can't get at a bakery anymore. It's well worth making at home!*

1/4 POUND (1 STICK) UNSALTED BUTTER

4 OUNCES UNSWEETENED CHOCOLATE

2 EGGS

1 2/3 CUPS SUGAR

2 CUPS ALL-PURPOSE FLOUR

PINCH OF SALT

1 1/2 TEASPOONS BAKING SODA

1 2/3 CUPS MILK

2 TEASPOONS VANILLA EXTRACT

Preheat the oven to 350° F. Butter two 9-inch round cake pans and dust generously with cocoa powder or flour.

Melt the butter and chocolate in a bowl set over a pot of simmering water. Meanwhile, beat the eggs with an electric mixer. Gradually add the sugar and beat until very light and a ribbon forms when the beaters are lifted. Stir the melted butter and chocolate together. Add the hot chocolate mixture to the eggs and beat to combine well.

Mix the flour and salt together; dissolve the baking soda in the milk. Stir the flour and milk into the chocolate-egg mixture in batches, beginning and ending with the flour. Stir in the vanilla. The batter will be rather thin.

Pour the batter into the pans and bake for 25 to 30 minutes, until a cake tester comes out clean. Cool for 5 minutes on a wire rack before turning out the cakes onto racks to cool completely.

Frost with chocolate frosting.

SERVES 10 TO 12

Chocolate Frosting

2 1/2 CUPS CONFECTIONERS'
SUGAR

1/3 CUP BEST-QUALITY COCOA

PINCH OF SALT

1/4 POUND (1 STICK)
UNSALTED BUTTER,
AT ROOM TEMPERATURE

1/2 TO 3/4 CUP HEAVY CREAM

1 TEASPOON
VANILLA EXTRACT

Sift the sugar, cocoa, and salt into the bowl of a standing mixer. Add the butter and cream well; the mixture will be very stiff.

Beat in enough cream to make a spreadable frosting. Beat in the vanilla.

MAKES ENOUGH FOR 1
TWO-LAYER CAKE

ABOVE LEFT AND LEFT. *Dessert has been set out on a Hoosier cabinet. The chocolate cake sits on a Buenilum hammered-aluminum stand. Other elements in the mix include old Anchor Hocking glass sandwich plates, Russel Wright silverplate forks and spoons, a Georg Jensen cake knife, and old restaurantware mugs.*

1

2 4

3

CENTERPIECES

They don't have to be simply flowers.

1. A brown paper lunch bag, its top rolled down and tied with a gold cord, becomes a container for breadsticks. **2.** The small Edwardian urn is filled with a nest of moss and combined with variegated acorn squash. **3.** This flea market treasure—an unusual pressed-metal candy dish—is piled high with quince from the green market. **4.** Another edible centerpiece: a cast-iron garden urn is filled with *grissini*. **5.** Here garden urns are filled with bunches of chive blossoms and fresh sage. Glass liners filled with water are set inside the urns. **6.** Dessert as centerpiece: a nosegay of long-lasting flowers and berries is nestled into a Bundt cake on a leaf-lined stand.

5

6

TABLES GO OUT ONTO THE

PORCH OR PATIO. THE MARKET AND THE GARDEN ARE OVERFLOWING WITH PRODUCE SO PRETTY IT DEMANDS TO BE THE CENTER OF THE TABLES. ❀ BEFORE WE PLANT FLATS OF YOUNG SALAD GREENS, WE LET THEM FILL A BASKET ON THE TABLE FOR A FEW DAYS. WE FILL OUR IRONSTONE PITCHERS WITH NEWLY CUT HERB BOUQUETS OR HANDFULS OF LOVAGE THAT SEEMS TO HAVE SHOT UP OVERNIGHT. ❀ WHEN ZUCCHINI TAKES OVER THE GARDEN, WE USE ITS GIANT LEAVES AS PLACE MATS AND ITS BLOSSOMS TO BRIGHTEN A SALAD. ❀ THE LUSH FRUITS OF SUMMER—MELONS, BERRIES, PEACHES, AND CHERRIES—LOOK PAINTERLY FILLING BOWLS AND BASKETS ON COUNTRY AND CITY TABLES. BUT THERE IS NOTHING THAT TASTES MORE DELICIOUS OR LOOKS PRETTIER ON A SUMMER TABLE THAN A PLATTER OF THICKLY SLICED RED AND YELLOW TOMATOES TOPPED WITH SPRIGS OF FRAGRANT BASIL. ❀ WHEN THE SETTING IS GREAT AND THE WEATHER WARM, YOU DON'T NEED TO DO MUCH TO ENHANCE THE TABLE. PERHAPS CHOOSE SIMPLE WHITE DINNER PLATES, AND LET LARGE LINEN DISHTOWELS OR TERRY WASHCLOTHS STAND IN FOR NAPKINS. KEEP IT ALL AS CAREFREE AND EASY AS A SUMMER BREEZE.

PICNIC IN A MEADOW

A meadow in the Berkshires, not far from the home of friends, tempted us to picnic. Lunch in a setting this beautiful really needs only some blankets to sit on, but we set out to transform the great outdoors into our dining room. We loaded up the old Jeep with table, chairs, sturdy plates and pressed-glass goblets, gingham cloths, and baskets full of food, and up the hill we went.

Baskets make the job of transporting and serving picnic fare much easier. One basket carried napkins and cutlery; the other—used to serve the cheeses—was lined with cut-out brown paper.

OPPOSITE. *Table and chairs have been moved out to the meadow for an ideal summer setting.* ABOVE. *A basket tray is lined with cut-out brown paper and filled with local goat cheese from Coach Farm. The twig knife handle is a replacement for the damaged original handle made of bone.*

Frittata in a Bread Box

A frittata is a delicious way to use leftover vegetables and meats, and still have a fresh and attractive main dish. Putting it in a bread "box" makes it easy to transport. We used a special loaf of Santa Fe bread from the Baker's Wife in Great Barrington, Massachusetts, but you can use any round loaf that's big enough. You can substitute any leftover vegetable you like for the zucchini, and feel free to add cooked sliced sausage, chicken, or ham.

1 12-INCH ROUND LOAF OF COUNTRY BREAD

$1/4$ CUP OLIVE OIL

4 GARLIC CLOVES, SLICED

2 CUPS ZUCCHINI, SLICED INTO $1/2$-INCH ROUNDS

1 CUP COOKED NEW POTATOES, SLICED $1/4$ INCH THICK

SALT AND BLACK PEPPER TO TASTE

12 EGGS

$1/4$ CUP MILK

1 CUP GRATED PARMESAN

Preheat the oven to 350° F.

Slice the bread in half lengthwise, and remove some of the soft center to create a "box" for the frittata. Wrap in heavy-duty foil and place in the oven for 15 to 20 minutes.

Meanwhile, heat the olive oil in a heavy 12-inch omelet pan. Add the garlic and sauté for 2 minutes. Add the zucchini, potatoes, and salt and pepper to taste, and continue to sauté for about 5 minutes.

Meanwhile, beat the eggs until frothy. Add the milk, $1/2$ cup of the Parmesan, and salt and pepper. Beat until well combined. Pour the eggs into the hot pan over the vegetables and cook on top of the stove until the eggs start to set, about 5 minutes. Sprinkle the top with the remaining Parmesan and then place the frittata in the oven. Cook for about 20 minutes, or until fully set.

Unwrap the bread. Run a knife around the sides of the pan to loosen the frittata, slide it into the bottom of the bread, put the top on, rewrap in the foil, and wrap it all in a pretty dishtowel until ready to serve.

SERVES 8

ABOVE. *Hobnail pressed-glass goblets are a good choice for an outdoor lunch; they're not only sturdy, but they sparkle in the noon light.* LEFT. *A market basket conveys food and tableware from home to picnic.*

SCREENED PORCH DINING

The screened porch overlooking the Catskill Mountains is the favorite summer setting for dinners at the home of Harriet and Bernie Shur.

Their dinners start as the sun begins to fade. The table is set with a mix of  blue-and-white transferware dinner plates, chunky pressed-glass goblets, and proper red-wine glasses—which are used here for white wine. Silverplate fiddle-pattern forks and spoons look comfortable with early-20th-century faux-bone-handled cutlery.

Flowers picked from Harriet's garden poke out of old cobalt-blue bottles at one end of the table. Down the middle, an old wooden bread-rising tray is filled with young local apples and vines, interfering with neither the conversation nor the view.

ABOVE. *Apples and vines in a wood bread-rising tray fill the length of the table.*
OPPOSITE. *The mixed pattern blue-and-white dinner plates are reproductions of antiques.*
OVERLEAF. *Harriet's tart, the pan wrapped in a napkin, rises to the view on a pressed-glass cake stand. A stack of Depression-glass dessert plates catches the glow of the late summer sun.*

Herb-Marinated Grilled Lamb

Have your butcher butterfly the lamb.

Marinade

¼ CUP DIJON MUSTARD

2 TABLESPOONS SOY SAUCE

4 GARLIC CLOVES, CRUSHED

1 TABLESPOON FRESH THYME LEAVES

¼ TEASPOON POWDERED GINGER

2 TABLESPOONS OLIVE OIL

1 LEG OF LAMB, BUTTERFLIED AND
WELL TRIMMED

Combine all the ingredients for the marinade in a bowl, blending well with a fork. Brush the marinade on both sides of the lamb, place it in a sealable plastic bag, and refrigerate overnight.

Allow the lamb to come to room temperature. Grill over hot coals until medium rare, about 8 minutes on each side. Let it rest for 5 minutes before slicing.

SERVES 4 TO 6

RIGHT. *Summer's bounty—beet greens, chard, baby carrots, string beans, and beets—adds vibrant color to the table.*

Harriet's Summer Tart

Use any berries in season for this tart.

1 ²/₃ CUPS UNBLEACHED ALL-PURPOSE FLOUR

¹/₄ CUP SUPERFINE SUGAR

¹/₂ TEASPOON SALT

10 TABLESPOONS BUTTER, CUT INTO SMALL BITS AND CHILLED

2 EGG YOLKS

1 TEASPOON VANILLA EXTRACT

2 TEASPOONS ICE WATER

1 JAR GOOD-QUALITY BERRY JAM

1 TABLESPOON FRAMBOISE (OR OTHER EAU-DE-VIE)

2 PINTS BLUEBERRIES

1 PINT STRAWBERRIES (OR ANY OTHER BERRIES IN SEASON)

Place the flour, sugar, and salt in the bowl of a food processor and pulse once or twice to mix. Add the butter and pulse until the mixture resembles oatmeal.

Beat together the egg yolks, vanilla, and ice water. Add to the flour mixture and process just until the pastry starts to form a ball.

Turn the pastry out into a 9-inch tart pan with a removable bottom and, with floured hands, press the pastry evenly into the pan. Cover with plastic wrap and refrigerate for at least 1 hour.

Preheat the oven to 425° F.

Prick the dough all over with a fork and bake for 20 minutes, until lightly browned. Set aside to cool.

Place the jam in a small pan and cook, stirring, over medium heat, until melted. Stir in the framboise, and push through a sieve.

Fill the tart shell with berries and glaze them with the jam.

SERVES 6

SUNFLOWER BUFFET

The galvanized flower pail, gray-green napkins, crisply patterned green-and-white plates, and silver cutlery set against weathered gray siding create a cool setting, punctuated by bright sunflowers and the hot salsa. Votive candles in plain, clear jigger glasses are ready to usher in the dusk.

ABOVE. *Classic martini glasses are just as glamorous when used for margaritas.*
OPPOSITE. *Four varieties of sunflower are piled into the galvanized flower pail.*

Chicken Fajitas

*A favorite for the summer buffet, especially when accompanied by
icy cold margaritas. Serve this with roasted corn salsa, guacamole, sour cream,
shredded sharp cheddar, chopped tomatoes, and a basket of
warm flour tortillas.*

Marinade

2 SHALLOTS, CHOPPED

1 LARGE ONION, CHOPPED

2 GARLIC CLOVES, MINCED

3 JALAPEÑO PEPPERS, SEEDS REMOVED AND CHOPPED

1 $1/2$ TEASPOONS BLACK PEPPER

$1/2$ TEASPOON CAYENNE PEPPER

2 TEASPOONS SALT

1 SMALL BUNCH OF CILANTRO, CHOPPED

1 $1/2$ CUPS DARK BEER

$1/2$ CUP CORN OIL

6 WHOLE BONELESS AND SKINLESS CHICKEN BREASTS

Combine all of the marinade ingredients in a shallow glass or porcelain bowl.

Add the chicken, cover, and refrigerate for several hours or overnight.

Prepare a grill and bring the chicken to room temperature. Remove the chicken from the marinade. Grill the breasts and slice them into strips.

SERVES   6

RIGHT. *The striped-border contemporary china becomes more interesting when paired and
stacked with wide-rimmed restaurant buffet plates.*

Roasted Corn Salsa

A great twist on an old favorite, the roasted corn adds a rich flavor.

6 EARS OF CORN, SHUCKED

6 TOMATOES, SEEDED AND CHOPPED

1 ONION, FINELY CHOPPED

1 SMALL BUNCH OF CILANTRO, FINELY CHOPPED

JUICE OF 2 LIMES

2 OR 3 JALAPEÑO PEPPERS, SEEDED AND FINELY CHOPPED

SALT AND BLACK PEPPER TO TASTE

Roast the corn over hot coals until lightly browned. Wrap in aluminum foil and leave on the grill another 10 to 15 minutes. Cut the kernels off the ears and place them in a large bowl.

Add the remaining ingredients and stir to combine. Cover and let the salsa sit at room temperature for at least an hour to allow the flavors to blend.

SERVES 6 TO 8

RIPE SUMMER FRUIT

In a beautiful garden created by Lisa Stamm, what could be more appropriate than grape leaves used as place mats? Perhaps the footed ceramic bowl filled with unripe grapes, leaves, and ripe summer fruit—a centerpiece of painterly quality that almost rivals the view.

OPPOSITE. *The French garden table and chairs are grouped to create an intimate setting in a large, open garden.* ABOVE. *Flea-market china is as at home on the table as the contemporary footed compote in sheer blue and green glazes.*

NIÇOISE LUNCH

When the setting is a garden in full bloom, like Phyllis and Charlie Rosenthal's, why compete? A wicker tray made it easy to carry napkins, goblets, and cutlery from the kitchen to the terrace. We added flowers picked on the spot to the focaccia-filled bread basket. And the salade Niçoise, artfully arranged on a large platter with sprigs of fresh thyme, made a centerpiece as pretty to look at as it was delicious to eat. Dark green glass plates provide a subtle background for lunch in this colorful garden.

OPPOSITE. *The salad is composed on a very large white ceramic platter.* ABOVE.
Unique, elaborately etched antique double old-fashioned glasses depict African animals.

Salade Niçoise

Fresh thyme is the secret ingredient that tastes like summer.

2 POUNDS THIN BABY GREEN BEANS,
BLANCHED UNTIL TENDER BUT CRISP

1 BUNCH CELERY, PALE,
INSIDE STALKS ONLY, CHOPPED MEDIUM-FINE

1 LARGE VIDALIA OR BERMUDA
ONION, CHOPPED MEDIUM-FINE

2 POUNDS SMALL NEW POTATOES,
CUT IN HALF AND BOILED IN SALTED WATER

1 PINT CHERRY TOMATOES

6 EGGS, BOILED ABOUT 6 MINUTES,
UNTIL WHITES ARE HARD,
CUT IN HALF

$1/_2$ POUND NIÇOISE OLIVES

SALT AND FRESHLY GROUND BLACK PEPPER

1 $1^1/_2$-POUND TUNA STEAK, ABOUT 1 $^1/_2$ INCHES THICK

OLIVE OIL

JUICE OF $^1/_2$ LEMON

1 2-OUNCE CAN OF FLAT ANCHOVY FILLETS

1 BUNCH OF GREEN ONIONS, CHOPPED

1 BUNCH OF THYME

VINAIGRETTE DRESSING (OPPOSITE)

On a large platter, arrange the green beans, celery, onion, potatoes, cherry tomatoes, eggs, and olives in pie-shaped wedges or in rows.

Salt and pepper the tuna on both sides. Preheat a skillet or grill to very hot.

Brush the tuna with olive oil and grill for 4 to 5 minutes on each side for a rare center, or until desired doneness.

Slice the tuna and place it in the middle of the platter on top of the vegetables. Sprinkle it with lemon juice. Garnish with anchovies. Sprinkle green onions and thyme leaves all over the platter. Serve with vinaigrette dressing.

SERVES 6

Vinaigrette Dressing

$1/4$ CUP DIJON MUSTARD

$1/4$ CUP TARRAGON VINEGAR

$1\,1/2$ TEASPOONS SALT

3 GARLIC CLOVES, FINELY MINCED

$1/2$ CUP OLIVE OIL

FRESH THYME LEAVES, CHOPPED

FRESHLY GROUND BLACK PEPPER

To make the vinaigrette, combine the mustard, vinegar, salt, and garlic. Add the olive oil, thyme, and pepper, and beat with a fork until well blended. Set aside.

ABOVE. *Dark green glass dinner plates and 1920s wood and Bakelite salad servers await.* LEFT. *Rolled jacquard napkins, stainless steel cutlery with riveted plastic handles, and sturdy faceted goblets in a basket tray: a good-looking solution to transporting tableware out of doors.*

A LAZY SUMMER MORNING

Only on a summer Sunday do we have the luxury of a leisurely breakfast outside. Half the fun is setting the table. We used cheery blue-and-white hand-painted ceramic dinner plates instead of place mats, with American spatterware dessert plates for the fruit, yogurt, and granola. A mix of blue-and-white patterned dishtowels makes user-friendly napkins.

ABOVE. *A carved wooden spoon is ready to serve granola, and a Thai teak and brass spoon is used for the yogurt.* OPPOSITE. *Hand-painted pottery, predominately blue, mixed with other blue-and-white tableware, is a great summer look against the verdant setting.*

LUNCH UNDER
AN ARBOR

An old-fashioned tablecloth on a garden table is a bit of a surprise, especially

when it's oversized, almost touching the ground. Everything on the table,

including the sauce, is the soft green that looks so perfect out of doors. The

setting and the shrimp club sandwich make lunch under the arbor a very

special event.

OPPOSITE. *A square tablecloth on a round table, the long points almost brushing the*
ground, make the arbor setting even more romantic. ABOVE. *A single sunflower sits in*
a vintage glass water dispenser.

Lisa's Green Sauce

2 EGGS

6 BUNCHES PARSLEY,
STEMS REMOVED, COARSELY
CHOPPED

$^1/_4$ CUP CAPERS

1 GREEN BELL PEPPER, SEEDED
AND FINELY CHOPPED

JUICE AND ZEST OF 1 LIME

4 GARLIC CLOVES, COARSELY
CHOPPED

2 CUPS EXTRA-VIRGIN OLIVE OIL

Bring a small pan of water to a gentle boil. Carefully lower the eggs in with a spoon. Cover the pan, remove it from the heat, and set it aside for 6 minutes.

Combine one egg and one egg yolk with the parsley, capers, bell pepper, lime juice and zest, and garlic. Process until well blended. With the motor running, drizzle in the oil.

Store in the refrigerator in a glass jar with a tightly fitting lid. The sauce can be kept for about a week.

MAKES ABOUT 4 CUPS

Shrimp Club
Sandwich

A delicious update of an old standby.

For each sandwich

2 THICK SLICES OF PEASANT BREAD

4 ARUGULA LEAVES

2 THICK SLICES OF RIPE TOMATO

3 LARGE COOKED SHRIMP,
SLICED IN HALF

2 STRIPS OF CRISP BACON

LISA'S GREEN SAUCE (OPPOSITE)

Place one slice of bread on the plate. Layer on the arugula, tomato, shrimp, and bacon. Top with the other slice of bread and serve with Lisa's green sauce on the side.

OPPOSITE TOP. *A Victorian silverplate tablespoon is waiting on a French park chair to serve Lisa's green sauce.* OPPOSITE BOTTOM. *When a tablecloth is too big, improvise—fold it to fit! The extra layers pad the table and add dimension.* ABOVE RIGHT. *Daisy Wolfman and Rose Gold would rather be eating shrimp than riding in the old green garden cart!* RIGHT. *This green-and-white spatterware plate is a new version of early American pottery.*

DINNER ON A TERRACE

The weekend at Lisa Stamm and Dale Booher's Shelter Island home was a feast for all of our senses. Their gardens are magnificent, their table settings creative, and their food delicious.

The walls of their house are covered with trellis and climbing roses. Well-placed mirrors reflect the views so that guests never feel as if they are facing in the wrong direction. A discarded and rusted drill bit, artfully entwined with ivy and angelonia, is at home on their terrace table. Purple peppers (a first for us) and baby eggplants were added just for this dinner.

The meal started with lobster and corn salad served over new potatoes. Green-and-white striped place mats were just the right background for the Portuguese basketweave plates, white liners, and etched green glass tumblers.

OPPOSITE. *The weathered table is the perfect foil for the setting.* ABOVE. *Daughter Vanessa Booher drew cartoons on porcelain place cards with a symbol for each guest.*

Lobster and Corn Salad

*We make this salad the day after a lobster and corn dinner,
which cuts the preparation time in half.*

Vinaigrette

2 TABLESPOONS DIJON MUSTARD

1 TEASPOON SUGAR

$1/3$ CUP FRESH LEMON JUICE

6 TARRAGON LEAVES, FINELY MINCED

SALT AND FRESHLY GROUND BLACK PEPPER TO TASTE

$2/3$ CUP OLIVE OIL

Salad

2 POUNDS NEW POTATOES, BOILED

1 LOBSTER (ABOUT 2 POUNDS), BOILED, WITH MEAT REMOVED

4 EARS OF CORN, ROASTED, WITH KERNELS REMOVED

1 CUP CHOPPED CELERY

1 CUP CHOPPED ONION

1 CUP SEEDED AND CHOPPED TOMATO

$1/4$ CUP MINCED FRESH TARRAGON LEAVES

SALT AND FRESHLY GROUND BLACK PEPPER TO TASTE

SPRIGS OF FRESH TARRAGON FOR GARNISH

Prepare the vinaigrette by combining the mustard, sugar, lemon juice, tarragon, and salt and pepper in a bowl. Whisk together as you drizzle in the oil.

To make the salad, cover the potatoes with cold salted water, bring to a boil, and cook until tender; drain and slice. Place the potatoes on a platter and drizzle them with enough vinaigrette to moisten.

Cut the lobster meat into bite-sized pieces and place them in a mixing bowl. Add the corn, celery, onion, tomato, tarragon, and salt and pepper and toss with the remaining vinaigrette.

Place a layer of the boiled potatoes on each plate, top with the lobster salad, and garnish with a sprig of tarragon.

SERVES 4

ABOVE. *Purple peppers and eggplants surround a rusted, ivy-entwined drill bit, filling the center of the long table.* LEFT. *The green of the Portuguese pottery, striped woven mats, and giant leaves makes a pleasing background for the colorful salad.*

LUNCH OVERLOOKING THE RIVER

Truly great settings, like this one on the Connecticut River, require very little in the way of table decoration. A few blueberry branches, ripe peaches, and—to mimic a Renaissance still life—a melon sliced and still filled with its seeds.

Everything about the setting speaks of a classical discipline: the view framed by hedges, the limestone terrace, the black iron table and chairs, and the crisp white linen napkins scalloped in black.

ABOVE. *The centerpieces of ripe summer fruit will be eaten for dessert.* OPPOSITE. *The simple, truly elegant setting.*

RIGHT. *Green peppers and branches of unripe blueberries make a spontaneous still life.* BELOW RIGHT. *Octagonal 19th-century faience creamware with black transfer figures was set atop simple restaurant plates.* OPPOSITE. *Lobster stew is served in a rolled-rim French restaurantware soup bowl* (TOP). *A platter of summer tomatoes and fruit from the garden of a friend* (CENTER). *A loaf of bread rests on one of a pair of 18th-century stone statues overlooking the river* (BOTTOM).

Not-Too-Rich Lobster Stew

1 SMALL WHITE ONION, CHOPPED

1 GARLIC CLOVE, CHOPPED

1/3 CUP MINCED CELERY AND LEAVES

2 TABLESPOONS BUTTER

1 CUP DRY VERMOUTH

1 CUP CHICKEN BROTH

1 TEASPOON THREAD SAFFRON

4 1 1/4-POUND UNCOOKED LOBSTERS, CUT INTO PIECES

1 CUP HEAVY CREAM, BLENDED WITH 2 TABLESPOONS FLOUR

SALT AND WHITE PEPPER

Sauté the onion, garlic, and celery in butter until tender, 5 to 6 minutes. Add the vermouth, chicken broth, and saffron. Bring to a boil. Add the lobster, cover, and simmer 5 to 6 minutes.

Stir in the cream mixture, and continue stirring until hot and thickened. Add salt and pepper to taste.

SERVES 4

Blackberry Dessert Pizza

To make this pretty and unusual dessert, use your favorite pizza dough recipe or buy the dough ready-made.

ZEST OF 1 LEMON

PIZZA DOUGH (HOMEMADE, SEE PAGE 134, OR STORE-BOUGHT)

$^1/_2$ CUP GRANULATED SUGAR

2 PINTS OF FRESH BLACKBERRIES (OR ANY BERRIES IN SEASON)

CONFECTIONERS' SUGAR

Preheat a pizza stone in a 400° F. oven.

Knead the lemon zest into the dough and let it rise until doubled. Divide into 4 equal balls and roll into circles about $^1/_2$ inch thick.

Sprinkle each round with granulated sugar.

Bake dough on a hot pizza stone for about 15 minutes, until golden brown.

Place on a serving plate and top with berries. Sprinkle generously with confectioners' sugar.

SERVES 4

RIGHT. *Even the silver tray is sprinkled with confectioners' sugar, making the dessert pizza look cool and inviting.*

AN ELEGANT
PIZZA LUNCH

At the elegant Connecticut home of our friends Carlene and Ed Safdie, the table appears quite formal, but on a closer look it becomes apparent that all of the elements are quite simple. A vintage white damask cloth is layered over the table skirt; large damask napkins are unfolded next to restaurant-ware buffet plates. Earthy terra-cotta pots hold glamorous white orchids and chilled wine. The surprise is that the thin-crust pizza, made with fresh vegetables and low-fat cheese, is served on a silver tray!

OPPOSITE. *White orchids set the tone in the white setting.* ABOVE. *Unfolded damask napkins and restaurant plates make an elegant setting a little less formal.*

Really Easy, Thin Crust Vegetable Pizza

In Florence they call it schiacciata, *a flat bread very much like focaccia.*
With this easy recipe, you can make great savory bread or pizza crust.
Flavors can be added to the dough by kneading in lemon zest,
roasted garlic, rosemary, pepper, black olives, or whatever suits the toppings.
You can use almost anything to top these little pizzas. Try the
chopped tomato salad that tops the pasta on page 79.
For a more traditional topping, smear a thick marinara sauce on
the unbaked dough and add chopped mozzarella and sautéed mushrooms or
sliced black olives sprinkled with fresh chopped basil.

1 PACKAGE ($\frac{1}{4}$ OUNCE) DRY ACTIVE YEAST

1 CUP LUKEWARM WATER

3 CUPS UNBLEACHED FLOUR, PLUS FLOUR FOR WORK SURFACE

$\frac{1}{4}$ CUP EXTRA-VIRGIN OLIVE OIL

FRESH ROSEMARY LEAVES

SALT

Dissolve the yeast in the water for about 10 minutes.

Combine the yeast with the flour. Knead the dough on a floured surface, gradually adding flour if necessary, until it no longer feels sticky.

Form the dough into a ball and place it in a floured bowl. Cover with a dish towel, set in a warm place, and let rise until doubled in size, about 1 hour.

Punch down the dough and divide into 4 equal pieces. With a rolling pin, roll each piece into a circle $\frac{1}{2}$ inch thick. Let it rise on a floured baking pan for 30 minutes.

Preheat a pizza stone in 400° F. oven.

Poke the surface of each pizza with your fingers, brush with oil, and sprinkle with rosemary and salt, or other topping. Bake for about 15 minutes, until golden brown.

MAKES 4 SERVINGS

LEFT. *A rolled-edge terra-cotta flowerpot makes a good summer wine cooler; the plate underneath will catch the melting ice.* BELOW LEFT. *A mushroom and a tomato-basil pizza share a silver fluted-edge tray.* ABOVE. *The salad is arranged in a white ceramic bowl.* BELOW. *A bottle made to hold both oil and vinegar shares a plate with a pair of antique silver salt and pepper shakers.*

OUT ON THE PORCH

This cozy screened porch is a great setting for a group of friends to share a messy seafood boil. Shrimp in the shell, crab, and corn on the cob are served from a giant crockery bowl. Unmatched wood candlesticks share the middle of the table with a jug of sunflowers, while very American spatterware plates wait to be filled.

A French hollow-handle silver salad spoon paired with an old American butter crock is as appealing and unlikely a combination as the blue cheese

and cabbage slaw. On the sideboard, a turned-wood cake stand lined with brown paper is filled with oatmeal cookies. Peaches and candied ginger marinate with mint in a hand-painted Italian bowl. In another vintage butter crock, iced champagne is ready and waiting to celebrate the end of a great summer meal.

ABOVE. *An old American yellowware batter bowl is filled to the brim with an East Coast seafood boil.* OPPOSITE. *The table is a riot of blue and green.*

Seafood Boil

*Use any combination of local and
seasonal seafood.*

4 CUPS WATER

1 BOTTLE OF DRY WHITE WINE

1 PACKAGE OF OLD BAY SEASONING

$1/2$ CUP MALT VINEGAR

4 GARLIC CLOVES, CUT IN HALF

SALT AND BLACK PEPPER TO TASTE

12 SMALL NEW POTATOES

6 CELERY STALKS,
CUT INTO 3-INCH LENGTHS

2 SWEET ONIONS, QUARTERED

6 LINKS CHORIZO,
CUT INTO 1-INCH ROUNDS

6 EARS OF CORN, BROKEN IN HALF

36 MEDIUM SHRIMP, CLEANED,
TAILS LEFT ON

6 CRABS OR SMALL LOBSTERS

Combine the water, wine, Old Bay, vinegar,
and garlic in a large stockpot. Bring to a boil,
lower the heat, and simmer for 5 minutes.
Add salt and pepper.

Add the potatoes and cook for 8 minutes.
Add the celery, onions, and sausage and simmer for another 8 minutes. Raise the heat,
bring to a boil, and add the corn and seafood.
Cook until the shells turn bright pink.

Pour into a large bowl and serve.

SERVES 6

Blue Cheese Slaw

A great twist on the usual coleslaw.

1 HEAD GREEN CABBAGE, SHREDDED

1 HEAD PURPLE CABBAGE, SHREDDED

1 SPANISH ONION, HALVED AND
SLICED THIN

2 CUPS RICE VINEGAR

3 TABLESPOONS SUGAR

1 TEASPOON SALT

$\frac{1}{2}$ POUND ROQUEFORT OR BLUE
CHEESE, BROKEN INTO PIECES

Combine all the ingredients but the cheese in a large ceramic bowl and stir well. Cover with a glass or porcelain plate smaller than the bowl, place a weight on the plate, and refrigerate for 1 hour.

Drain off all the liquid, toss in the cheese, and serve.

SERVES 6

OPPOSITE TOP. *The pale green glass flutes were made in Mexico from old Coca-Cola bottles.* OPPOSITE BOTTOM. *Extra-large gingham napkins are pulled through antique numbered ivory napkin rings.* ABOVE RIGHT. *The turned-wood plate stand is lined with a circle of brown paper and filled with cookies.* RIGHT. *French silver-handled salad servers poke out of the blue cheese slaw in the stoneware butter crock.*

Peaches with Candied Ginger and Mint

The flavor of ginger is a natural with peaches, but the crunch of the candied ginger is a real taste treat. This is delicious spooned over a scoop of vanilla ice cream.

6 PEACHES, PEELED AND SLICED

1 PINT BLUEBERRIES

JUICE OF 1 LEMON

$^1/_2$ CUP MINCED CANDIED GINGER

$^1/_4$ CUP CHOPPED FRESH MINT LEAVES

$^1/_2$ TEASPOON VANILLA EXTRACT OR RUM

Combine all the ingredients in a glass or porcelain bowl, cover, and let stand for about 1 hour to let the flavors blend.

SERVES 6

RIGHT. *An Italian terra-cotta bowl, glazed inside but unglazed out, holds ripe summer peaches with ginger. Another versatile butter crock is used to chill champagne.*

FOUR SETTINGS

1. Lace-edged cotton piqué napkin made by Flossi, tied with gold cord. American ceramic buffet plate; gold-rimmed Limoges dinner plate made by Haviland; vintage Wedgwood drabware lunch plate. French silverplate cutlery. **2.** Flat eucalyptus leaves and berries cover the table. Stoneware buffet plate by Boda Nova made in Sweden; "Candlewick" glass dinner plate by Dalzell Viking; Chinese rice bowl. French silverplate "Vieux Paris" cutlery. Mexican short-stemmed etched goblet. **3.** Old rose sepia-print tablecloth made by La Serviette in New York. Limoges buffet and salad plates designed by Billy Goldsmith; raised-pattern Italian ceramic dinner plate; Revere-style glass bowl from Tiffany. Faceted old-fashioned glass by Baccarat. **4.** Cotton print tablecloth with border, made by Karen Lee Ballard. Vintage Queen Anne–style ceramic buffet plate; hand-made ceramic dinner plate and soup bowl by Aletha Soule. French plastic-handled stainless steel cutlery by Scoff.

directory

Though there are many vintage and antique pieces shown in the settings and on the tables in this book, few are one-of-a-kind. With a bit of hunting through antiques shops (some listed in the directory) and flea markets, similar pieces can usually be found.

This directory is provided as a service. The information herein was accurate at the time of publication.

ARIZONA

CORNELIA PARK

Biltmore Fashion Park
2474 East Camelback Road
Phoenix, AZ 85016
602-955-3195
602-553-8380 fax

Colorful hand-painted English-style pottery and furniture, glassware, linens, and a selection of antique silver Victorian cutlery. MacKenzie-Childs Collection. One of the few shops in this part of the country with no Southwestern merchandise.

DOS CABEZAS

The Borgata
6166 N. Scottsdale Road
Suite 300
Scottsdale, AZ 85253
602-991-7004
602-483-9781 fax

Brightly colored Mexican pottery, painted enamel plates, hand-etched glasses, candlesticks, and one-of-a-kind handmade silver serving pieces.

DUPUIS

Biltmore Fashion Park
2468-A East Camelback Road
Phoenix, AZ 85016
602-912-0177
602-912-0179 fax

Neutral and white Mexican pottery, silver and wood candlesticks. Wood, silver, and ceramic oversized serving pieces, generous etched goblets, wine and champagne glasses.

THE IMPECCABLE PIG

7042 East Indian School Road
Scottsdale, AZ 85251
602-941-1141

Antique and contemporary tableware including pottery, Mexican glassware, rustic linens, candlesticks, gourmet foods, and Southwestern accessories.

NORTHERN CALIFORNIA

AMERICAN PIE

3101 Sacramento Street
San Francisco, CA 94115
415-929-8025

Candles, fine candy, bath goods (soaps, lotions), frames, and books.

CARMEL BAY COMPANY

Box 5606
Ocean Avenue and Lincoln Street
Carmel, CA 93921
408-624-3868

Contemporary and rustic things for the table in a mostly neutral palette. Pottery, dinnerware, straw and natural-fiber place mats and napkins, chunky glassware, and baskets. Pine dining furniture.

FILLAMENTO

2185 Fillmore
San Francisco, CA 94115
415-931-2224
415-931-6304 fax

The cutting edge of style in tableware: handmade ceramics, mouth-blown glass, natural-fiber napkins and place mats, silver-plate and stainless-steel cutlery, candles, candlesticks. Also contemporary furniture.

FORREST JONES, INC.

3274 Sacramento Street
San Francisco, CA 94115
415-567-2483
415-567-7604 fax

Informal dinnerware, pottery, bowls, and platters. Bistro flatware, table linens, and a large collection of baskets.

THE GARDNER

1836 Fourth Street
Berkeley, CA 94710
510-548-4545 and 510-548-4564

Craftsman-made pottery, glasses, and cutlery. Intriguing, earthy vases, bowls, and accessories. Wood dining tables with stone or galvanized tops, outdoor tables and chairs.

GREBITUS & SONS

511 L Street
Downtown Plaza Center
Sacramento, CA 95814
916-442-9081
916-442-3950 fax
and
2850 Fairoaks Boulevard
Lyon Village Center
Sacramento, CA 95815
916-487-7853
916-487-0912 fax

Antique silver, china, crystal, flatware.

JUDITH ETS-HOKIN HOMECHEF

3525 California Street
San Francisco, CA 94118
415-668-3191
415-668-0902 fax

Cooking school and store specializing in professional cookware, whiteware, stoneware, bowls, platters, basic linens, and cookbooks.

MACY'S

170 O'Farrell Street
San Francisco, CA 94102
415-397-3333

A large selection of cookware, gourmet foods, and tableware, including platters, bowls, dinnerware, linens, candles, and picnic baskets.

MOSSWOOD

1239 Main Street
St. Helena, CA 94574
707-963-5990
707-963-5009 fax

Hand-painted pottery, candles, candlesticks, and decorative and garden accessories.

R H

2506 Sacramento Street
San Francisco, CA 94115
415-346-1460

Oversized tableware, platters, Italian pottery, American ceramics, wood-handled flatware, and topiary herbs.

SIGN OF THE BEAR

435 First Street West (on the
   Square)
Sonoma, CA 95476
707-996-3722 phone and fax

A country store with table- and kitchenware; specializing in local California pottery.

SUE FISHER KING

3067 Sacramento Street
San Francisco, CA 94115
415-922-7276
415-922-9241 fax

Italian and French ceramic dinnerware, glassware, and flatware. An extensive selection of natural-fiber tablecloths, napkins, and place mats and fine imported linens.

TIFFANY & CO.

350 Post Street
San Francisco, CA 94108
415-781-7000
415-296-0760 fax

Fine selection of china, crystal, sterling flatware, and table accessories.

TURNER MARTIN

540 Emerson Street
Palo Alto, CA 94301
415-324-8700
415-324-1611 fax

Decorative ceramic bowls and platters, candles and candle holders.

VANDERBILT & CO.

1429 Main Street
St. Helena, CA 94574
707-963-1010

A large and colorful selection of country and contemporary pottery and china, napkins and napkin rings, tablecloths and place mats, silverplate and stainless cutlery, and glassware.

VIVANDE PORTA VIA

2125 Fillmore Street
San Francisco, CA 94115
415-346-4430
415-346-2877 fax

Gourmet picnic baskets, imported food, cookbooks, cafe.

WILLIAMS-SONOMA

150 Post Street
San Francisco, CA 94108
415-362-6904
415-362-2852 fax

Catalogue and stores have an international collection of basic tableware, including whiteware, dinnerware, platters, bowls, bar- and stemware, stainless flatware, and basic linens, cookware, and specialty foods.

SOUTHERN CALIFORNIA

THE BLUE HOUSE

8440 Melrose Avenue
Los Angeles, CA 90069
213-852-0747 phone and fax
and
1402 Montana Avenue
Santa Monica, CA 90403
310-451-2243 phone and fax

Importers of English and French antiques, specializing in blue and white Staffordshire transferware and antique cutlery.

CINZIA

1129 Montana Avenue
Santa Monica, CA 90403
310-393-7751

Italian and provincial dinnerware, fine table linens, and decorative accessories.

FERRET

12334 Ventura Blvd.
Studio City, CA 91604
818-769-2427
818-769-0904 fax

Elegant tableware, including Chinese blue-and-white bowls, reproduction majolica, terra-cotta, and French porcelain, table linens, and napkin rings.

GAZEBO ANTIQUES

120 South Robertson Boulevard
Los Angeles, CA 90048
310-275-5650
310-475-1442 fax

Eighteenth- and nineteenth-century English and Irish pine furniture, country French furniture, old and new imported and domestic baskets, blue-and-white china.

GEARY'S

351 North Beverly Drive
Beverly Hills, CA 90210
310-273-4741
310-858-7555 fax

China, crystal, silver, linens, cookware.

HOLLYHOCK

214 North Larchmont Blvd.
Los Angeles, CA 90004
213-931-3400
213-463-1248 fax

An ever-changing collection of antique china, linens, and flatware. Old colored glass and English ceramics.

LINENS, ETC.

20929 Ventura Blvd.
Woodland Hills, CA 91364
818-702-8895

Odd-size and custom-made linens, place mats, candles, baskets, and some French dinnerware.

PICCOLO PETE'S ART DECO STORE

13814 Ventura Boulevard
Sherman Oaks, CA 91423
818-907-9060
818-990-5421 fax

Art Deco vintage dinnerware, Fiestaware, pressed glass, barware, and Bakelite cutlery.

PORT O'CALL

906 Granite Drive
Pasadena, CA 91101
818-796-7113
818-796-2254 fax

Baccarat crystal, Christofle silver, fine china, place mats, pottery, and antique tableware.

SHAXTED

350 North Camden Drive
Beverly Hills, CA 90210
310-273-4320
310-273-8067 fax

Imported and domestic table linens and accessories.

TIFFANY & CO.

210 North Rodeo Drive
Beverly Hills, CA 90210
310-273-8880
310-273-6766 fax

Fine china, crystal, sterling flatware, and table accessories.

COLORADO

AMEN WARDY

405 East Cooper Avenue
Aspen, CO 81611
970-920-7700
970-920-9163

From contemporary to classic; a colorful and deep selection of china, hand-painted pottery, stemware, cutlery, and more than 400 patterns in table linens.

ANNIE'S

100 East Meadow Drive
Building 2
Vail, CO 81657
970-476-4197

Baccarat crystal, Christofle flatware, Herend, Waterford fine china, baskets, cookbooks.

A PLACE ON EARTH

141 East Meadow Drive
Vail, CO 81657
970-476-1118 phone and fax

Table accessories handcrafted by American artisans.

HOMEFEST

123 North College Avenue
Fort Collins, CO 80524
970-221-5069
970-495-9930 fax

From country to formal; china includes majolica and Quimper. Sterling and stainless flatware. Table linens from France, Italy, and Asia.

INTERNATIONAL VILLA

262 Fillmore Street
Denver, CO 80206
800-759-9696
303-333-5954 fax

Baccarat and Lalique crystal, sterling flatware, and fine traditional china.

KRISMAR, LTD.

100 East Meadow Drive
Vail, CO 81657
970-476-3603
970-476-1348 fax

Kitchenware, traditional cookware, table linens, cutlery, fine china, barware, and gourmet coffees.

CONNNECTICUT

BRITISH COUNTRY ANTIQUES

50 Main Street North (Route 6)
Woodbury, CT 06798
203-263-5100

Antique plate racks and furniture, earthenware and stoneware serving dishes, wood and metal kitchenware, baskets, pitchers.

CHURCH STREET TRADING

19 Church Street
New Milford, CT 06776
203-355-2790

Country pottery, French bistro ware, handwoven rugs, willow furniture.

COOK'S BAZAAR

400 Crown Street
New Haven, CT 06511
203-865-5088
203-865-2731 fax

Contemporary cookware and tableware, gourmet foods.

HAY DAY

1050 East Putnam Avenue
Riverside, CT 06878
203-637-7600
203-698-1360 fax
and
1026 Post Road East
Westport, CT 06880
203-254-5200 phone and fax

Country market including platters, baskets, gourmet foods.

JANE COTTINGHAM ANTIQUES

PO Box 3001
Newtown, CT 06470
203-426-4000

Antiques by appointment.

LYNNENS, INC.

278 Greenwich Avenue
Greenwich, CT 06830
203-629-3659
203-629-3993 fax

*Custom-made bed, bath, and table
linens: Palais Royal, Anichini, Bellino,
and Madeira.*

QUIMPER FAÏENCE

141 Water Street
Stonington, CT 06378
860-535-1712
860-535-3509 fax

*Devoted exclusively to the provincial
hand-painted earthenware of
Quimper, France.*

THE SILO

44 Upland Road
New Milford, CT 06776
203-355-0300
203-350-5495 fax

Food, kitchenware, tableware.

THE TRUMPETER, INC.

5 Main Street, Box 2490
New Preston, CT 06777
203-868-9090
203-868-9929 fax

*Antique tableware, silver cutlery,
silver food domes.*

THE WRITE APPROACH

1306 Whalley Avenue
New Haven, CT 06515
203-397-8272
203-387-1482 fax

*Hand-loomed place mats and napkins,
baskets, antique fish sets, hand-
painted Portuguese platters, gourmet
foods, cookbooks, Italian pottery.*

DISTRICT OF COLUMBIA

CHERISHABLES

1608 20th Street, N.W.
Washington, DC 20009
202-785-4087
202-785-7335 fax

*Eighteenth- and nineteenth-century
American country furniture and
accessories, contemporary cottons,
linens, porcelain, and antique tableware.*

DEAN & DELUCA

3276 M Street, N.W.
Washington, DC 20007
202-342-2500
202-342-2525 fax

*Classic French whiteware; platters,
bowls, pitchers, and dinnerware. Bistro
flatware, sturdy glasses, basic table
linens, and professional cookware.*

KITCHEN BAZAAR

4401 Connecticut Avenue, N.W.
Washington, DC 20008
202-244-1550
202-244-9653 fax

*International cookware and dinner-
ware, spices, baskets, picnic ware.*

FLORIDA

BASKETVILLE

4411 South Tamiami Trail
Venice, FL 34293
813-493-0007
813-492-6789 fax

*Baskets, buckets, pottery, wooden uten-
sils, rustic place mats and napkins.*

KASSATLY'S

250 Worth Avenue
Palm Beach, FL 33480
407-655-5665
407-835-9808 fax

*Custom-made tablecloths and place
mats, ready-made European table
linens.*

LUMINAIRE

2331 Ponce de Leon Boulevard
Coral Gables, FL 33134
305-448-7367
305-448-9447 fax

*Contemporary housewares, European
flatware, glassware.*

NESSA GAULOIS

9700 Collins Avenue
Bal Harbour, FL 33154
305-864-3226
305-865-4801 fax

*China, crystal, flatware, linens, French
stainless-steel cookware.*

OUR WAREHOUSE

301 Northeast 36th Street
Oakland Park, FL 33334
305-565-2867
305-563-7496 fax

*Restaurant-supply dinnerware and
foods, including Villeroy and Boch
china, Porcelaine d'Auteuil, Reidel
and Orrefors glassware, a selection of
800 wines, caviars, imported cheeses.*

THE UNPRESSURED COOKER,
INC.

32 Periwinkle Place
Sanibel, FL 33957
813-472-2413

Chantal cookware and cookbooks.

GEORGIA

BALLARD DESIGNS

1670 Defoor Avenue
Atlanta, GA 30318
404-352-8486
404-352-1660 fax

Tabletop accessories.

ERIKA READE

3718 Roswell
Atlanta, GA 30342
404-233-3857

*An eclectic collection of new and
antique pottery, French and Italian
table linens, and Scottish crystal.*

PERIDOT

514 East Paces Ferry Road N.E.
Atlanta, GA 30305
404-261-7028

*Table linens, glassware, accessories,
candlesticks, and candles.*

TABBY HOUSE

105 Retreat Road
St. Simons Island, GA 31522
912-638-2257

*Antique serving ware, table acces-
sories, furniture.*

TIFFANY & CO.

Phipps Plaza
3500 Peachtree Road N.E.
Atlanta, GA 30326
404-261-0075
404-264-9807 fax

*Fine china, crystal, sterling flatware,
and table accessories.*

IDAHO
CABIN FEVER

113 Cedar Street
Sandpoint, ID 83864
208-263-7179
208-265-5188 fax

*Porcelain, pottery, and ceramics from
around the world; table linens; and
pewter serving pieces.*

ILLINOIS
ADESSO

600 Central Avenue
Highland Park, IL 60035
708-433-8525

*Handmade porcelain, ceramic, and
earthenware platters, bowls, and dinnerware. Table linens, hand-blown
glass, and stainless flatware.*

ART EFFECT

651 West Armitage
Chicago, IL 60614
312-664-0997
312-664-5421 fax

*Colorful handmade pottery made by
American artists.*

CRATE & BARREL

646 North Michigan Avenue
Chicago, IL 60611
312-787-5900

*Catalogue and stores have a large
array of clean, contemporary mostly
white china, platters, and bowls.
Sturdy barware and more delicate
stemware. Stainless-steel flatware and
basic napkins and place mats.*

ELEMENTS

102 East Oak Street
Chicago, IL 60611
312-642-6574

*Nontraditional ceramics and pottery.
Hand-blown glassware, linens, and
flatware.*

FINDABLES

907 West Armitage
Chicago, IL 60614
312-348-0674

*Colorful ceramic dinnerware and
platters, glassware and flatware.
French and Italian linens.*

LUMINAIRE

301 West Superior Street
Chicago, IL 60610
312-664-9582
312-664-5045 fax

*Contemporary housewares, European
flatware, kitchen accessories.*

MATERIAL POSSESSIONS

954 Green Bay Road
Winnetka, IL 60093
847-446-8840
847-446-8843 fax

*Handmade ceramic dinnerware and
glassware, table linens, and flatware.*

TABULA TUA

1015 West Armitage
Chicago, IL 60614
312-525-3500
312-281-9301 fax

*Contemporary imported and domestic
art ceramics, specializing in serving
bowls and platters. Custom table
linens, European and American flatware, and unique tabletop accessories.*

TIFFANY & CO.

715 North Michigan Avenue
Chicago, IL 60611
312-944-7500
312-664-6107 fax

*Fine china, crystal, sterling flatware,
and table accessories.*

INDIANA
M. G. TATES

8702 Keystone Crossing
Indianapolis, IN 46240
317-846-4273
317-846-3701 fax

*Kitchenware, cookbooks, crystal,
flatware, china, linens.*

IOWA
CELLA CELLARS

408 5th Street
West Des Moines, IA 50265
515-279-4995
515-279-1037 fax

*Pottery from Italy, Portugal, England,
and America. French and Belgian
table linens, and primitive American
furniture.*

DUCK SOUP

116 South Market Street
Ottumwa, IA 52501
515-682-9583 phone and fax

Tableware, china, crystal, cookbooks.

THE EGG SHELL

255 Valley West Mall
West Des Moines, IA 50266
515-223-5778
515-223-4745 fax

*High-tech kitchenware, glasses,
cannister sets.*

KITCHENWORKS

155 Collins Road N.E.
Cedar Rapids, IA 52402
319-393-0710

*Functional kitchenware, cookware,
gourmet foods.*

THE PEPPER MILL

Southern Hills Mall
Sioux City, IA 51106
712-276-9043 phone and fax

Tableware and kitchenware, cookbooks, baskets.

KANSAS
NELLHILL'S

501 Commercial Street
Atchison, KS 66002
913-367-1086
913-367-3821 fax

Baskets, kitchenware, furniture, rugs.

THE PAPER PLATE

4018 West 83rd Street
Prairie Village, KS 66208
913-341-7701
816-931-9636 fax

Paper goods, plastic cutlery, cookbooks.

LOUISIANA
COLEMAN ADLER'S

722 Canal Street
New Orleans, LA 70130
504-523-5292
504-568-0610 fax

Traditional and contemporary dinnerware, cookware.

JAY ARONSON, LTD.

200 Broadway, Suite 132
New Orleans, LA 70118
504-865-1186
504-865-1187 fax

Traditional china, crystal, and silver.

LUCULLUS

610 Chartres Street
New Orleans, LA 70130
504-528-9620
504-561-8030 fax

Antique tableware; china, including dinnerware, platters, tureens, and pitchers. Pressed glass and crystal, sterling and silverplate flatware, and linens.

NATALEE

331 Heymann Blvd.
Lafayette, LA 70503
318-233-5000
318-237-9307 fax

A mix of fine china, Mexican pottery, English crystal, baskets, and unusual home and garden accessories.

WOK & WHISK

6301 Perkins Road
Baton Rouge, LA 70808
504-769-5122
504-769-9285 fax

Informal china and glassware, kitchenware, baskets, cookbooks.

MAINE
MAINE'S MASSACHUSETTS HOUSE

Route 1
Lincolnville, ME 04849
207-789-5705
207-789-5707 fax

Traditional handcrafted stoneware and table linens.

MARYLAND
STEBBINS ANDERSON

802 Kenilworth Drive
Towson, MD 21204
410-823-6600
410-321-6078 fax

Informal dishes, linens, kitchenware. Patio furniture.

THE STORE, LTD.

Village of Cross Keys, #24
Baltimore, MD 21210
410-323-2350

Contemporary tableware, cookware, baskets, ceramic crocks.

MASSACHUSETTS
BASKETVILLE

416 Main Street
West Dennis, MA 02670
508-394-9677
508-394-3475 fax
and
419 Main Street
Sturbridge, MA 01566
508-347-3493
508-347-2971 fax

Baskets, buckets, pottery, wooden utensils, rustic place mats and napkins.

CHURCH STREET TRADING

4 Railroad Street
Great Barrington, MA 01230
413-528-6120

THE COUNTRY DINING ROOM ANTIQUES

178 Main Street
Great Barrington, MA 01230
413-528-5050
413-528-9216 fax

An extensive collection of antique tableware; sets of china from Staffordshire to Minton, pressed glass to cut crystal. Sets of Victorian silver serving and dining cutlery all displayed on antique dining tables and hutches. Plus a good selection of new table linens and napkin rings fine enough to stand up to the antiques.

CRATE & BARREL

140 Faneuil Hall Marketplace
Boston, MA 02109
617-742-6025
617-742-5197 fax

Catalogue and stores have a large array of clean, contemporary mostly white china, platters, and bowls. Sturdy barware and more delicate stemware. Stainless-steel flatware and basic napkins and place mats.

KITCHENARTS

161 Newbury Street
Boston, MA 02116
617-266-8701
617-266-6300 fax

Cookware, bakeware, cutlery, cook-books. Special orders.

LA RUCHE

168 Newbury Street
Boston, MA 02116
617-536-6366
617-536-8424 fax

French porcelain, ceramics, and color-fully patterned pottery. Custom table linens, glassware, candles, and candle-sticks.

THE LION'S PAW

Box 1817
0 Main Street
Nantucket, MA 02554
508-228-3837
508-228-6821 fax

Painted pottery, glassware, painted furniture, traditional linens, china, flatware, and housewares.

O'RAMA'S

148 Washington Street
Marblehead, MA 01945
617-631-0894

Antique and one-of-a-kind contempo-rary linens and dinnerware.

T. P. SADDLE BLANKET & TRADING CO.

304 Main Street
Great Barrington, MA 01230
413-528-6500
413-528-6370 fax

Cowboy china, tin mugs and coffee pots, cutlery and drinking glasses. Oversized napkins made of chambray, checks, and plaids with eyelet trim, and baskets to tote them all in.

MICHIGAN
GATTLE'S

Lake and Howard Streets
Petoskey, MI 49770
616-347-3982
616-347-3987 fax

Table linens.

HORN OF PLENTY

442 South Woodward Avenue
Birmingham, MI 48009
810-645-2750
810-645-5760 fax

Contemporary and traditional dinner-ware, stainless flatware, glasses, bas-kets, cookware, linens. Food, fruit, and wine baskets.

JOHN LEIDY SHOP

601 East Liberty Street
Ann Arbor, MI 48104
313-668-6779
313-668-6935 fax

Contemporary and traditional china, stoneware, crystal, flatware, linens, cookware.

KITCHEN GLAMOR

26770 Grand River
Redford, MI 48240
313-537-1300
313-537-0111 fax

Cookbooks and kitchenware.

KITCHEN PORT

415 North Fifth Avenue
Ann Arbor, MI 48104
313-665-9188
313-665-8052 fax

Cookware, kitchenware, dinnerware, baskets, cookbooks.

ORTHOGONALITY

205 North Woodward Avenue
Birmingham, MI 48009
810-642-1460

Dinnerware, candles, baskets, house-wares, glassware.

SEASONS

5100 Marsh Road
Okemos, MI 48864
517-349-8400
517-349-8402 fax

Casual furniture and dinnerware, paper goods and plastic cutlery, candles, baskets, cookbooks.

MINNESOTA
AMPERSAND

5034 France Avenue South
Edina, MN 55410
612-920-2118
612-920-2148 fax

Imported and domestic pottery, ceramics, and porcelain. Crystal and hand-blown glass, French and Italian linens.

DAYTON'S

700 On the Mall
Minneapolis, MN 55402
612-375-2200
612-375-2027 fax

White dinnerware, glassware, casual table linens, cookware, flatware, cookbooks.

FIVE SWANS

309 East Lake Street
Wayzata, MN 55391
612-473-4685
612-473-4686 fax

Dinnerware, cookware, linens, paper goods, giftware.

PROVISIONS

320 Water Street
Excelsior, MN 55331
612-474-6953
612-474-0875 fax

Baskets, casual table linens, paper goods, cookbooks, candles, white dinnerware.

MISSOURI
HALLS CROWN CENTER

200 East 25th Street
Kansas City, MO 64108
816-274-8111
816-274-4471 fax

Contemporary kitchenware.

HALLS PLAZA

211 Nichols Road
Kansas City, MO 64112
816-274-3222
816-274-3220 fax

Traditional china, crystal, flatware.

SALLIE

9821 Clayton Road
St. Louis, MO 63124
314-567-7883
314-567-7248 fax

Fine china, crystal, table linens, flatware, candles.

NEW JERSEY

DINING IN

2 West Northfield Road
Livingston, NJ 07039
201-992-8300

American handcrafted pottery, glass, baskets, floral arrangements, handcrafted napkin rings.

EAGLE'S NEST

Country Mile Route 202
Morristown, NJ 07960
201-425-1372
201-425-0221 fax

Traditional and antique china, gourmet food, table linens, baskets.

PLATYPUS

Princeton Market Fair
3535 US Highway 1
Princeton, NJ 08540
609-734-9377
and
The Grove at Shrewsbury
611 Route 35
Shrewsbury, NJ 07702
908-758-0100

Tableware, kitchenware, gourmet food, baskets.

TABLE OF CONTENTS

58 East Palisade Avenue
Englewood, NJ 07631
201-567-3355
201-567-2007 fax

Contemporary china, crystal, flatware, table linens, place mats, and accessories.

NEW MEXICO

DESIGN WAREHOUSE

101 West Marcy Street
Santa Fe, NM 87501
505-988-1555
505-473-1539 fax

Casual furniture, tableware, linens, and cookware.

MONET'S KITCHEN

124M Bent Street
Taos, NM 87571
505-758-8003
505-758-5478 fax

Cooking and baking accessories, gourmet foods, cutlery, glassware, and table linens.

PENNYSMITH'S

4026 Rio Grande Boulevard, N.W.
Albuquerque, NM 87107
505-345-2383
505-344-8595 fax

Paper goods, baskets, platters, candelabras, candles, handcrafted New Mexican table accessories.

TAOS COOKERY

113 Bent Street
Taos, NM 87571
505-758-5435

Local pottery and other handmade items, table linens, cutlery, cookware, New Mexican specialty foods.

NEW YORK CITY

ABC CARPET & HOME

888 Broadway
New York, NY 10003
212-473-3000
212-995-9474 fax

A grand bazaar of a store filled with all styles of tableware, including china, pottery, glassware, crystal, table linens, and cutlery.

AD HOC SOFTWARES

410 West Broadway
New York, NY 10012
212-925-2652
212-941-6910 fax

Contemporary china, glassware, flatware, and natural-fiber table linens.

BARNEYS NEW YORK

Seventh Avenue and 17th Street
New York, NY 10011
212-593-7800
and
660 Madison Avenue
New York, NY 10021
212-826-8900

Colorful contemporary ceramics and handmade glass. French and Italian table linens. A fine collection of late-19th- and early-20th-century pottery.

BERGDORF GOODMAN

754 Fifth Avenue
New York, NY 10019
212-753-7300
212-872-8616 fax

Fine china and handmade ceramic dinnerware, crystal, fine linens, serving pieces, and silver cutlery.

BLOOMINGDALE'S

1000 Third Avenue
New York, NY 10022
212-355-5900

Varied assortment of tableware, kitchenware, cookware, decorative accessories, candles, and baskets.

BRIDGE KITCHENWARE

214 East 52nd Street
New York, NY 10022
212-688-4220
212-758-5387 fax

Professional tableware and kitchenware, including French and American restaurant whiteware, serving pieces, barware, and stainless-steel cutlery.

CERAMICA

59 Thompson Street
New York, NY 10012
212-941-1307

Italian ceramics, hand-painted with traditional centuries-old designs. As in the shops in Italy, the platters, plates, pitchers, coffee cups, and bowls are boldly colored and patterned.

CRATE & BARREL

650 Madison Avenue
New York, NY 10020
212-308-0011
212-843-0943 fax

Catalogue and stores have a large array of clean, contemporary, mostly white china, platters, and bowls. Sturdy barware and more delicate stemware. Stainless-steel flatware and basic napkins and place mats.

DEAN & DELUCA

560 Broadway
New York, NY 10012
212-431-1691
212-334-6183 fax

Classic French whiteware; platters, bowls, pitchers, and dinnerware. Bistro flatware, sturdy glasses, basic table linens, and professional cookware.

FELISSIMO

10 West 56th Street
New York, NY 10019
212-247-5656
212-956-0081 fax

Porcelain, handmade ceramics, and glassware influenced by nature. Rustic place mats, tablecloths, and napkins.

FISHS EDDY

889 Broadway
New York, NY 10003
212-420-9020
212-353-1454 fax
and
2176 Broadway
New York, NY 10024
212-873-8819
212-873-4169 fax

A shop filled with new and old china with logos of restaurants, hotels, country clubs, and schools. The shapes are suitable for everything from soup to nuts, morning coffee to espresso.

GRACIOUS HOME

1220 Third Avenue
New York, NY 10021
212-517-6300
212-249-1534 fax

Everything for the home, including a selection of basic tableware, paper plates and napkins, votive candles and holders, and plumbers' candles.

HENRI BENDEL

712 Fifth Avenue
New York, NY 10019
212-247-1100
212-397-8519 fax

Frank McIntosh; ever-changing and colorful assortment of table linens, contemporary flatware, glassware, ceramics, and accessories.

HOWARD KAPLAN ANTIQUES

827 Broadway
New York, NY 10003
212-674-1000
212-228-7204 fax

Unique English and French country antique and reproduction dining tables, buffets, cupboards, chairs, and lighting fixtures.

JAMES ROBINSON, INC.

480 Park Avenue
New York, NY 10022
212-752-6166
212-754-0961 fax

Handmade sterling silver flatware. Place settings can include as many as 25 pieces. Tea and coffee services, fine antique silver, porcelain, and glass.

LAMALLE KITCHENWARE

36 West 25th Street
New York, NY 10010
212-242-0750
212-645-2996 fax

A loft shop filled with fine cookware, copper pots, pastry tools, and molds.

VICTORIA AND RICHARD MACKENZIE-CHILDS, LTD.

824 Madison Avenue
New York, NY 10021
212-570-6050
212-570-2485 fax

Multi-patterned and highly colored handmade majolica dinnerware, stemware, linens, and furniture, all with the unmistakable MacKenzie-Childs look.

MACY'S CELLAR

131 West 34th Street
New York, NY 10001
212-695-4400

A large assortment of basic tableware, cookware, and gourmet foods.

SUSAN P. MEISEL DECORATIVE ARTS

133 Prince Street
New York, NY 10012
212-254-0137
212-533-7340 fax

Early-20th-century art pottery; includes Clarice Cliff.

MOOD INDIGO

181 Prince Street
New York, NY 10012
212-254-1176

One of the largest collections of Art Deco tableware, including Fiestaware, vintage Hall china, Russel Wright dinnerware, stainless-steel cocktail shakers and barware. Plus novelty salt and pepper shakers and a good selection of Bakelite cutlery.

SIMON PEARCE

385 Bleecker Street
New York, NY 10014
212-924-1142
and
212-243-0203 fax
500 Park Avenue
New York, NY 10022
212-421-8801
212-421-8802 fax

Bold and beautiful hand-blown glass goblets, tumblers, bowls and pottery with the Simon Pearce signature and look.

PIERRE DEUX

870 Madison Avenue
New York, NY 10021
212-570-9343
212-472-2931 fax

French country cotton table linens, dinnerware, baskets, antiques.

TAKASHIMAYA

693 Fifth Avenue
New York, NY 10022
212-350-0100
212-350-0192 fax

An artful combination of Eastern and Western tableware; Japanese laquerware, Murano glass, and French porcelain. Domestic and Asian linens, and a large selection of chopsticks and chopstick rests.

TIFFANY & CO.

727 Fifth Avenue
New York, NY 10022
212-755-8000
212-605-4152 fax

A fine selection of china, crystal, sterling flatware, and table accessories.

PAMELA SCURRY'S WICKER GARDEN

1318 Madison Avenue
New York, NY 10128
212-410-7000
212-410-7119 fax

Antique and reproduction wicker tables, chairs, high chairs, trays, and baskets; antique tablecloths and napkins.

WILLIAM WAYNE & CO.

846 Lexington Avenue
New York, NY 10021
212-737-8934
212-288-8915 fax
and
40 University Place
New York, NY 10003
212-533-4711
212-533-4730 fax

New and antique gifts, accessories, and furniture: monkeys a favorite motif.

WOLFMAN·GOLD & GOOD COMPANY

117 Mercer Street
New York, NY 10012
212-431-1888
212-226-4955 fax

White and cream dinnerware from England, France, Portugal, China, and Italy. Handmade ceramics in earthy neutrals from American potters. An extensive collection of antique silverplate Victorian cutlery. Silverplate and stainless bistro flatware, table linens, paper doilies, glassware, large serving platters and bowls, slip-covered couches and chairs.

ZABAR'S

2245 Broadway
New York, NY 10024
212-787-2000
212-580-4477 fax

Gourmet foods, cookware, and kitchenware.

ZONA

97 Greene Street
New York, NY 10012
212-925-6750
212-941-1792 fax

Southwestern, Mexican, and Italian pottery, glassware, linens, and silver for the table. Dining tables of painted wood, tile, and metal.

NEW YORK STATE
BALASSES HOUSE ANTIQUES

Main Street and Hedges Lane
Amagansett, NY 11930
516-267-3032
516-267-1048 fax

Antique and reproduction country tables, chairs, armoires, and buffets. New and antique earthenware, platters, pitchers, glasses, and silverplate cutlery.

ENGLISH COUNTRY ANTIQUES

Snake Hollow Road
Bridgehampton, NY 11932
516-537-0606
516-537-2657 fax
and
21 Newtown Lane
East Hampton, NY 11937
516-329-5773

An extensive collection of antique pine dining tables, sideboards, and chairs, plus Staffordshire platters and pitchers, silverplate cutlery sets and serving pieces.

CLIFFHANGERS

66 Pondfield Road
Bronxville, NY 10708
914-793-2397

Rugs, painted wood furniture, folk art accessories, decorative tabletop accessories, table linens.

CONSIDER THE COOK

Yellow Monkey Village
Route 35
Cross River, NY 10518
914-763-8844
914-763-8845 fax

A country store with tableware, cookware, glassware, linens, cookbooks, and baskets.

C & W MERCANTILE

Main Street
Bridgehampton, NY 11932
516-537-7914

French jacquard linens, rag and dhurrie rugs, handmade pottery, baskets, and candles. European and American table linens, flatware, and glassware.

ENGEL POTTERY

51 Main Street
East Hampton, NY 11937
516-324-6462 phone and fax

International selection of baskets of all shapes and sizes. African and Asian table accessories.

THE GILDED CARRIAGE

95 Tinker Street
Woodstock, NY 12498
914-679-2607 phone and fax

Gourmet kitchenware, dinnerware, linens, baskets, hand-painted Italian pottery, paper doilies, exceptional paper goods (plates, napkins).

KITCHEN CLASSICS

Main Street
Bridghampton, NY 11932
516-537-1111

A colorful selection of ceramic dinnerware, place mats, serving pieces, flatware, and table linens.

POSITIVELY MAIN STREET

773 Elmwood Avenue
Buffalo, NY 14222
716-882-5858

Contemporary table accessories, table linens, baskets, serving pieces.

RICHARD CAMP ANTIQUES

Montauk Highway
Wainscott, NY 11975
516-537-0330

Antique and reproduction stripped country pine tables. Vintage china, platters, and cutlery.

YELLOW MONKEY ANTIQUES

Route 35
Cross River, NY 10518
914-763-5848
914-763-8832 fax

Large selection of stripped pine tables, chairs, hutches, sideboards, and table accessories.

NORTH CAROLINA

CIEL

601 Providence Road
Charlotte, NC 28207
704-372-3335
704-372-9890 fax

Handmade ceramics, glassware, silverplate and stainless flatware. Locally made country pine and painted tables.

GRODZICKI & CO.

611 Providence Road
Charlotte, NC 28207
704-334-7300
704-334-7380 fax

China, linens, doilies, crystal.

THE METRO

911 East Morehead Street
Charlotte, NC 28204
704-375-4563
704-375-8220 fax

A broad selection of contemporary tableware, including china, stainless flatware, glassware, and serving pieces.

NORTH DAKOTA

CREATIVE KITCHEN

West Acres
Fargo, ND 58103
701-282-8694
701-282-0182 fax

Cookware, specialty foods, glassware, gadgets, cookbooks, cutlery.

OHIO

A. B. CLOSSON, JR., CO.

401 Race Street
Cincinnati, OH 45202
513-762-5519
513-762-5515 fax

Dinnerware, cookware, cookbooks, picnic ware, flatware, crystal, contemporary serving pieces.

GATTLE'S

3456 Michigan Avenue
Cincinnati, OH 45208
513-871-4050
513-871-4331 fax

Traditional table linens, MacKenzie-Childs tableware.

THE PANHANDLER

2724 Erie Avenue
Cincinnati, OH 45208
513-321-8062
513-321-8290 fax

Contemporary tableware and cookware, baskets, cookbooks, coffees and teas.

POTTER AND MELLEN

10405 Carnegie Avenue
Cleveland, OH 44106
216-231-5100
216-231-5104 fax

English and French dinnerware, Baccarat crystal, antique and reproduction silver, gourmet cookware, linens.

QUAILCREST FARM

2810 Armstrong Road
Wooster, OH 44691
216-345-6722
216-345-3842 fax

Baskets, cookbooks, casual linens, paper goods and picnic baskets, fresh herbs and herb wreaths, hand-thrown pottery.

OREGON

CLOUDTREE & SUN

112 North Main Street
Gresham, OR 97030
503-666-8495

*Gourmet cookware and tableware,
fine linens, gourmet foods.*

KITCHEN KABOODLE

Progress Square Shopping Center
8788 S.W. Hall Boulevard
Portland, OR 97223
503-643-5491

*Cookware, dinnerware, linens, baskets,
cookbooks, and furniture.*

PENNSYLVANIA

BASKETVILLE

Route 30
Paradise, PA 17562
717-442-9444 phone and fax

*Baskets, buckets, pottery, wooden uten-
sils, rustic place mats and napkins.*

CHEF'S BAZAAR

Routes 501 and 322
Lititz, PA 17543
717-627-0614

*Hand-thrown pottery, cutlery, linens,
and cookbooks.*

KITCHEN KAPERS

213 South 17th Street
Philadelphia, PA 19103
215-546-8059 phone and fax

*Contemporary and country cookware;
porcelain, glassware, cookbooks.*

THE LINEN KORNER

820 South Aiken Avenue
Pittsburgh, PA 15232
412-621-5600
412-687-9313 fax

*Domestic linens and linens imported
from Italy, Ireland, and Madeira.*

RHODE ISLAND

RUE DE FRANCE

78 Thames Street
Newport, RI 02840
401-846-2084
401-846-6821 fax

*French lace place mats and table
runners, Provençal pottery.*

SOUTH CAROLINA

BASKETVILLE

4350 Highway 501 West
Myrtle Beach, SC 29578
803-236-5555 phone and fax

*Baskets, buckets, pottery, wooden uten-
sils, rustic place mats and napkins,
silk flowers, wicker furniture.*

SOUTH DAKOTA

LARSEN DESIGNS, LTD.

1608 Southwestern Avenue
Sioux Falls, SD 57105
605-336-6037
and
544 Main Street
Spearfish, SD 57783
605-642-9301

*Paper goods, kitchenware, candles,
baskets, coffees.*

TENNESSEE

THE LINEN STORE

4045 Hillsboro Road
Nashville, TN 37215
615-383-6062
615-383-6013 fax

*Traditional china, glassware, table
linens, cookware, Herend porcelain,
Spode china, crystal.*

TEXAS

THE CONTAINER STORE

6060 Forest Lane
Dallas, TX 75230
214-386-5054
and
3060 Mockingbird Lane
Dallas, TX 75205
214-373-7044
214-761-2413 fax
and
1522 North Collins
Lincoln Square Shopping Center
Arlington, TX 76011
817-277-4448
817-277-7824 fax

Wire shelving.

CRATE & BARREL

220 North Park Center
Dallas, TX 75225
214-696-8010
214-696-3480 fax
and
Dallas Galleria
13350 Dallas Parkway
Suite 1650
Dallas, TX 75240
214-392-3411
214-392-2841 fax
and
Galleria—No. 2300
5175 Westheimer
Houston, TX 77056
713-621-7765
713-621-5860 fax

*Catalogue and stores have an array
of clean, contemporary, mostly white
china, platters, and bowls. Sturdy barware and more delicate stemware.
Stainless-steel flatware and basic napkins and place mats.*

EAST & ORIENT COMPANY

1123 Slocum Street
Dallas, TX 75207
214-741-1191
214-741-2192 fax

Antique tableware and fine linens.

JONES AND JONES

2100 South 10th Street
McAllen, TX 78503
210-687-1171
210-687-5013 fax

*Tableware, kitchenware, linens,
antiques, baskets, paper goods.*

TIFFANY & CO.

The Dallas Galleria
13350 Dallas Parkway
Dallas, TX 75240
214-458-2800
214-980-0629 fax
and
The Houston Galleria
5015 Westheimer Road
Suite 2100
Houston, TX 77056
713-626-0220
713-877-8120 fax

*Fine selection of china, crystal, sterling
flatware, and table accessories.*

VERMONT
BASKETVILLE

P.O. Box 710, Route 5
Putney, VT 05346
802-387-4351
802-387-5235 fax

*Baskets, buckets, pottery, wooden uten-
sils, rustic place mats and napkins.*

F. H. GILLINGHAM & SONS

16 Elm Street
Woodstock, VT 05091
802-457-2100
802-457-2101 fax

*One hundred-year-old New England
general store with "everything from
caviar to manure."*

SIMON PEARCE

The Mill
Quechee, VT 05059
802-295-2711
802-295-2853 fax

*Bold and beautiful hand-blown glass
goblets, tumblers, bowls, and pottery
with the Simon Pearce signature and
look.*

T.P. SADDLE BLANKET & TRADING CO.

Routes 11 and 30
Manchester Center, VT 05255
802-362-9888
802-362-3042 fax

VIRGINIA
BASKETVILLE

Route 60
Toano, VA 23168
804-566-8420

*Baskets, buckets, pottery, wooden uten-
sils, rustic place mats, napkins, and
silk flowers.*

GALE GOSS COUNTRY FRENCH ANTIQUES, INC.

1607 Colley Avenue
Norfolk, VA 23517
804-625-1211
804-625-0071 fax

French antiques, fine china, and gifts.

QUIMPER FAIENCE

1121 King Street
Alexandria, VA 22314
703-519-8339 phone and fax

*French provincial hand-painted
earthenware of Quimper.*

WASHINGTON
DOMUS

141 Bellevue Square
Bellevue, WA 98004
206-455-2728
206-455-2535 fax

*Contemporary dinnerware and table
linens.*

MR. "J" KITCHEN GOURMET

10116 N.E. 8th Street
Bellevue, WA 98004
206-455-2270
206-451-1578 fax

*Cookware, dinnerware, linens, paper
goods.*

OPUS 204

225 Broadway East
Seattle, WA 98102
206-325-1781
206-325-6647 fax

*Untraditional white china, Italian
glassware, imported crystal, baskets,
Chinese blue-and-white serving bowls,
Baltic tableclothes, napkins, African
napkin rings.*

SUR LA TABLE

84 Pine Street
Pike Place Farmer's Market
Seattle, WA 98101
206-448-2244

*Selection of gourmet cookware, dinner-
ware, bowls, platters, and cutlery.
Table linens.*

WISCONSIN
PERCY'S

11041 North Port Washington
  Road
Mequon, WI 53092
414-241-9343
414-241-9364 fax

*Custom-made table linens, china,
crystal, cookbooks, table accessories.*

POTPOURRI

2500 North Mayfair Road
Mayfair Mall
Wauwatosa, WI 53226
414-475-0033
414-475-1307 fax
and
5900 North Port Washington Road
Bayshore Mall
Milwaukee, WI 53217
414-332-0033

*Contemporary stoneware, glassware,
kitchenware, baskets, cookbooks,
porcelain.*

TELLUS MATER

409 State Street
Madison, WI 53703
608-255-7027

*Contemporary glassware, china, cook-
ware, baskets, linens.*

CATALOGUES AND NATIONAL STORES

The stores listed here are well known and are in most major cities. They have comprehensive catalogues illustrating their wares. For a catalogue or the store nearest you, call their 800 number.

BALLARD DESIGNS

404-351-5099
404-352-1660 fax

Catalogue only; dining tables, slipcovered chairs, tablecloths, plate stands, and up-to-the-moment accessories.

CRATE & BARREL

800-323-5461
708-215-0482
847-215-0482 fax

Catalogue and stores have a large array of clean, contemporary, mostly white china, platters, and bowls. Sturdy barware and more delicate stemware. Stainless-steel flatware and basic napkins and place mats.

GUMP'S

800-284-8677
800-945-9042 fax

Catalogue and stores have a good selection of fine tableware, including china, crystal, sterling flatware, linens, and Oriental antiques.

THE HORCHOW COLLECTION

800-456-7000
214-401-6414 fax

Catalogue only; always-changing selection of tableware and home furnishings.

POTTERY BARN

800-922-5507
415-421-5153 fax

Catalogue and stores have an evolving collection of sophisticated informal tableware; china, earthenware, glassware, flatware, and linens.

SUR LA TABLE

800-243-0852
206-682-1026

Catalogue and store (one store in Seattle) are known for a broad and professional selection of cookware, French bistro dinnerware, bowls, platters, and cutlery.

TIFFANY & CO.

800-526-0649
800-421-4468

Catalogue and stores have fine china, crystal, sterling flatware, and table accessories.

WILLIAMS-SONOMA

800-541-2233
415-421-5153 fax

Catalogue and stores have an international collection of basic tableware, including whiteware, dinnerware, platters, bowls, barware and stemware, stainless flatware, and basic linens, cookware, and specialty foods.

index